# SEVERN VALLEY
# RAILWAY

**One of** the Severn Valley Railway's very popular 'Santa Specials' heading purposefully back to Bewdley after an encounter with Father Christmas at Arley Station. *(Adrian White)*

# SEVERN VALLEY RAILWAY

Michael A. Vanns

PEN & SWORD
TRANSPORT

First published in Great Britain in 2017 by
Pen & Sword Transport
An imprint of Pen & Sword Books Ltd
47 Church Street
Barnsley
South Yorkshire
S70 2AS

Copyright © Michael A. Vanns, 2017

ISBN 978 1 47389 204 0

Printed and bound by Replika Press Pvt. Ltd

Typeset in Palatino

Pen & Sword Books Ltd incorporates the imprints of Pen & Sword
Archaeology, Atlas, Aviation, Battleground, Discovery, Family History,
History, Maritime, Military, Naval, Politics, Railways, Select, Social
History, Transport, True Crime, and Claymore Press, Frontline Books,
Leo Cooper, Praetorian Press, Remember When, Seaforth Publishing
and Wharncliffe.

For a complete list of Pen and Sword titles please contact:
Pen and Sword Books Limited
47 Church Street, Barnsley, South Yorkshire S70 2AS, England
E-mail: enquiries@pen-and-sword.Companyuk
Website: www.pen-and-sword.Companyuk

# Contents

# Introduction

Worcestershire and Shropshire are neighbours, and for 101 years until 1963 it was possible to travel by train between the two county towns of Worcester and Shrewsbury. For much of the journey, passengers would have been within sight of the River Severn, and it was a company deriving its title from that river that constructed the stretch of railway between Hartlebury and Shrewsbury at the end of the 1850s. This Severn Valley Railway was taken over by the West Midland Railway before the line opened, and a little over a year and a half later it became part of the Great Western Railway (GWR). That Company ran it for almost eighty-five years until all the country's railways were nationalised in 1948. British Railways continued to run trains over the whole route for another fifteen years before abandoning the section north from Bewdley to Shrewsbury. Fortunately, a new Severn

**A brief stop** at Buildwas Junction during the Shropshire Rail Tour of 23 May 1955. In the background are two of the six chimneys of the electricity power generating station. *(R. J. Buckley)*

**Cressage Station** as it appeared in the years immediately before the outbreak of the First World War. *(Author's collection)*

Valley Railway Company was formed by railway enthusiasts and by 1984 they were running steam-hauled trains between Kidderminster and Bridgnorth, having created one of the nation's most popular heritage attractions.

This book provides a brief history of the Severn Valley Railway from its earliest days through to the twenty-first century, providing a guide for all those who love the sight and sound of steam engines making their way through a particularly beautiful part of the Midlands landscape.

**Duchess of Sutherland** pulling away from the Sterns speed restriction on its way southwards, 21 September 2013. *(Author)*

# Genesis

For centuries the River Severn was an important trade artery, navigable by various craft from the Bristol Channel as far north as Welshpool to the west of Shrewsbury. In the eighteenth century it was of vital importance in the growth of both coal mining and the iron industry in the East Shropshire Coalfield, an area stretching from Donnington to the north of the river and Broseley to the south. The river provided the best means of exporting coal, pig iron and other cast and wrought-iron products. By the end of the 1750s the largest concentration of blast furnaces in the country was

**Benthall viaduct** close to the River Severn at Ironbridge, the famous cast-iron bridge just visible in the background. During the summer, when water levels were invariably low as shown here, river traffic almost ceased as boats could not negotiate the shallows. By comparison, a railway was a far more reliable means of transport whatever the weather. *(Ironbridge Gorge Museum Trust)*

**Detail of** an Edwardian postcard of the Iron Bridge looking east. To the right is Ironbridge & Broseley Station, on the opposite side of the River Severn to the town it served. In the background is the 'Free Bridge', opened without a toll in 1909. The chimney in the foreground marks the site of a brickworks. *(Commercial postcard/author's collection)*

immediately north and south of the river around Broseley and Coalbrookdale. When the Iron Bridge was erected over the river in 1779 to connect these two areas, it became, very appropriately, *the* symbol of England's industrial pre-eminence. Visitors, both legitimate and as spies, came from all over Europe to see it and marvel at the many industries in the vicinity. Even Thomas Jefferson, the third President of the USA, purchased a print of the bridge to hang in his Washington residence.

The industrialists in the East Shropshire Coalfield were also responsible for ground-breaking improvements in the way goods were moved between where they were made and the river. One of the earliest references to a railway appears in a legal document of 1605 that mentions a line of rails between Broseley and the River Severn. In the 1720s, the Coalbrookdale Company cast the country's first iron wheels and then began to lay cast-iron rails to replace wooden tracks in the 1760s. At the end of the century another form of railway was introduced into the area, often referred to as a 'plateway', on which the wagons' wheels were guided along the line by a continuous upright flange on each rail. Horse-drawn railway lines and plateways of various gauges criss-crossed the coalfield, linking mines, quarries and ironworks on both sides of the River Severn. The reputation of the area for its railways, and the casting and finishing of precision parts for Boulton & Watt steam engines attracted men such as Richard Trevithick, who in 1802 had the Coalbrookdale Company construct the very first steam engine designed to run on rails – plateway rails. Sadly, this engine did not receive the same publicity as his Penydarren engine that ran successfully two years later. Trevithick's involvement in Shropshire, however, did not end with the Coalbrookdale engine. In 1808 he returned to Bridgnorth where at Hazeldine's Foundry his last railway locomotive was built, destined to be considered little more than a fairground ride, when as 'Catch-me-who-can' it ran on a circle of track close to where Euston Station would later be located in London.

As well as developments in early railways, the East Shropshire Coalfield was also the location of innovative canal engineering. By the end of the eighteenth century, north of the river, the Coalfield was served by a network of 'tub-boat'

canals, the southern extremity reaching the river at Coalport via an inclined plane whilst the western end stretched to Shrewsbury.

This tub-boat canal system remained unique to Shropshire. Elsewhere in Britain, canals were constructed for narrow-boat operation and, although outside their area, it was one of these waterways that was to directly benefit the entrepreneurs of the Coalfield. In 1772 the Staffordshire & Worcestershire Canal opened between Great Haywood on the Trent & Mersey Canal and a junction with the River Severn a few miles south of Bewdley. At that junction a new settlement of 'Stourport' arose which very quickly starved Bewdley of much of its river trade, plunging that once-prosperous town into a state of suspended animation. That town's decline contrasted with a new opportunity for the entrepreneurs of the East Shropshire Coalfield because the

**The Coalport China Works** had been established at the end of the eighteenth century to take advantage of connections to both the River Severn and the Shropshire Canal, and it prospered because of those links. Nevertheless, as this note of 16 October 1863 bears witness, the Works' proprietor, John Rose, was quick to use the new Severn Valley Railway to dispatch items from his factory at Coalport to his shop in Shrewsbury. (Author's collection)

canal opened up a faster route into the Black Country for their pig iron and forge iron. Having reached the River Severn either along one of the cast-iron railways or over the tub-boat canal network to the river interchange at Coalport, the iron travelled down the Severn to Stourport and then on into the Black Country by canal.

The establishment of a china and porcelain works at Coalport in 1796 also reinforced the continuing importance of the river. The new factory was deliberately sited so that coal for its kilns could be delivered by tub-boat canal, and its supply of Cornish china clay could come in by river. John Rose's Coalport Works quickly benefitted from this careful planning to become

one of Britain's prestigious ceramics manufacturers alongside Minton, Wedgwood and Worcester.

Inevitably, the pioneering years of the eighteenth century when the East Shropshire Coalfield was at the forefront of industrial development could not last. The early years of the nineteenth century proved a difficult period for the iron industry in the Coalfield, with river traffic also in decline. By 1830 all the blast furnaces around Broseley had been abandoned. Iron ore mined in the south of the Coalfield continued to be exported via the River Severn to furnaces in Staffordshire and Worcestershire, but for industries north of the river, the completion of the Birmingham & Liverpool Junction Canal in 1835, and its northern link with the Shropshire tub-boat system, gave them a more reliable outlet for their goods than via the River Severn.

Interestingly, as the ironworks in the north of the Coalfield made less

**A view** of Coalport Station, from where John Rose's consignment of 1863 was dealt with. Until 1896 there would have been only one platform (on which the main buildings stood), but this view looking towards Bridgnorth shows the Station as it appeared a few years before the beginning of the First World War. *(Commercial postcard/author's collection)*

use of the river, the loss of traffic was compensated for by an increase in the carriage of bricks and roofing tiles from the Broseley and Jackfield areas to destinations both up and down stream. Consequently, although the River Severn was no longer as important as it had been to the iron trade, it remained busy at the beginning of Queen Victoria's reign. Although the East Shropshire Coalfield was no longer at the cutting edge of technological developments, it nevertheless continued to be an important industrial centre and maintained its considerable historic reputation. Unsurprisingly, therefore, when plans for a standard-gauge railway along the valley of the river were proposed during the 'Railway Mania' of 1845/6, the railway companies' prospectuses stressed the advantages of building lines to serve 'the mineral districts' of Ironbridge (the settlement that had grown up around the cast-iron bridge there), Coalbrookdale and Broseley.

## The first railway plans

In 1845 the Oxford & Worcester Extension & Chester Junction Railway (OWE&CJR) unveiled its scheme. The initial aim was to build a line from the planned Oxford, Worcester & Wolverhampton Railway (OW&WR) at Worcester, northwards along the river valley to Ironbridge where the main line would cross the Severn and head up the Coalbrookdale valley, through the heart of the East Shropshire Coalfield, and then onwards to Chester. From Ironbridge a 'branch' would follow the river to Shrewsbury. After further deliberations, the route through the Coalfield was shifted eastwards so as to avoid the difficult section through Coalbrookdale, and the branch to Shrewsbury was abandoned altogether.

What is particularly interesting about the changes made to this railway's plans is the light they shed on where the truly remunerative trade routes were perceived to be at the time. The River Severn may once have been important all the way from Worcester to Shrewsbury, but the OWE&CJR obviously believed there was nothing to be gained financially from building a railway between Ironbridge and Shrewsbury. The best return on any investment was felt to lie in linking Worcester with the East Shropshire Coalfield.

The other railway that had an interest in the Severn Valley was the Shropshire Union Railway & Canal Company (SUR&CC). This organisation was the result of a series of amalgamations. In

**Detail from** a pre-First World War Railway Clearing House map of the railways of Great Britain.
*(Author's collection)*

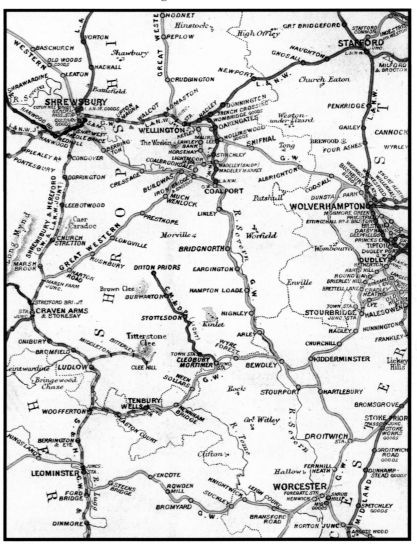

1845 the Ellesmere & Chester Canal Company merged with the Birmingham & Liverpool Junction Canal, and the SUR&CC title was adopted the following year when the Shropshire tub-boat canals were absorbed. In 1847 the Montgomeryshire Canal eastern branch was taken over, followed in 1850 by the western branch. By then the SUR&CC was considering the conversion of some of this canal network into railways as well as the construction of completely new lines. It planned a railway between Shrewsbury and Stafford, and like its rival the OWE&CJR, it also looked to build a new line from Worcester, through Bewdley and Bridgnorth to Coalport. From there the railway would continue up the same valley as the OWE&CJR planned to use, running through the Coalfield to link up with the planned Shrewsbury and Stafford line. In 1846 Robert Stephenson and his assistant, Frederick Swanwick, undertook a new survey for the Company that included three additional 'branches'. The first was to connect Stourport with Kidderminster; the second from Coalport to Shrewsbury where it was to join the projected Shrewsbury & Birmingham Railway (S&BR); and the third leaving the second branch just beyond Ironbridge, crossing the river into Coalbrookdale and continuing through the Coalfield to make another connection with the S&BR close to Oakengates.

Such was the manoeuvring in the Railway Mania period that neither the SUR&CC or the OWE&CJR's plans survived intact. The latter was dissolved at the end of 1846, and Parliament also refused to sanction the SUR&CC plans for its Severn Valley line and branches. The Company's bid to reach Stafford, however, was successful, although it was forced to collaborate with the S&BR in building a joint line between Shrewsbury and Wellington, from where the two

organisations could part company, the former driving its own line north-east to Stafford, and the latter continuing eastwards to Wolverhampton and Birmingham (although that last section was actually completed by another company).

In 1847 the SUR&CC was leased by the London & North Western Railway (LNWR), destined to become the most powerful railway company in the country, retaining its independence until 1923. The SUR&CC's line between Shrewsbury and Stafford was opened in June 1849, followed a little later in November by the rest of the S&BR to Wolverhampton. As stated above, the emphasis of transport in the East Shropshire Coalfield had already turned northwards away from the river, and the opening of these lines only reinforced that trend. If there were to be any new rail access into the Coalfield, then logically this would be achieved by running branches southwards from either the SUR&CC or the S&BR, rather than branches from an as-yet unbuilt railway running along the Severn Valley. Although the S&BR Act included authorisation for just such a branch, the Company had not exercised those powers.

Nevertheless, within a few years attention turned once again to a riverside railway and in 1849 a survey was carried out by Robert Nicholson, who had worked with Robert Stephenson. Unlike Stephenson's route for the SUR&CC, a much shorter section was to utilise the river valley. The aim was to build a railway from the OW&WR (still not finished, and earning a nick-name of the 'Old Worse and Worse'), not at Worcester, but a few miles further north at Hartlebury, following the river to Bridgnorth where it would cross to the east side and then abandon the valley altogether to make its way northwards to

**A connection** with the Oxford, Worcester & Wolverhampton Railway (OW&WR) at Hartlebury became the aim of the Severn Valley Railway in its Acts of 1853, 1855 and 1858. The junction was finally created just north of the passenger station where this later standard GWR sign was located. *(Author's collection)*

Madeley where it would connect with the S&BR's authorised branch (mentioned above).

There were obviously doubts about Nicholson's plans and the proposals were not pushed forward with any urgency. When a company was eventually formed in 1852 to build a new railway between Worcestershire and Shropshire, its very name – the Severn Valley Railway Company (SVR) – indicated plans had changed once again. Much of Stephenson and Swanwick's 1846 route had been re-adopted, bringing the line back into the river valley and taking it on from Bridgnorth, not overland to Madeley, but alongside the Severn through Ironbridge to Shrewsbury. Unfortunately, this met with implacable opposition from the Conservative MP for Bridgnorth, Thomas Charlton Whitmore, whose country seat was at Apley Park just north of that town.

As he did not want to see trains from his house, the railway had to agree to build a series of tunnels to hide their passage near his estate. To compensate for this unnecessary civil engineering work, Stephenson's tunnel under Bridgnorth was to be avoided by crossing the river south and north of the town. The railway was to be double-track with a branch into Coalbrookdale (requiring another bridge across the river) and with powers to connect with the proposed Wellington & Severn Junction Railway (W&SJR). planning to reach that same spot from the north with a branch off the S&BR at Ketley. The SVR's Bill went through the Parliamentary Committee stages in the summer of 1853 and emerged little altered, receiving the Royal Assent on 20 August that year.

In June the following year the S&BR opened its 'Coalbrookdale' branch, this single-track line leaving the main line almost midway between Oakengates and Shifnal stations, skirting the eastern fringes of the East Shropshire Coalfield to Lightmoor, where the Coalbrookdale Company operated blast furnaces, and where traffic could be exchanged with

the existing plateway network. Within three months, this branch, along with the rest of the S&BR, was absorbed into the Great Western Railway (GWR), another nationally-powerful company that survived until 1947.

By then the SVR was struggling to raise sufficient funds for its plans, and was looking to make economies with yet more route adjustments. After further discussions with Whitmore, a new alignment closer to the river was agreed that eliminated the tunnels opposite Apley Park. At Shrewsbury, instead of a connection to the Shrewsbury & Chester Railway (S&CR), an agreement was reached with the Shrewsbury & Hereford Railway (S&HR) to form a junction with its line and run trains into the proposed joint station to be built for all the railways serving the town. The route was modified

**The SVR** was fortunate in having the services of John Fowler as its engineer after 1854 because Victoria Bridge, Arley, seen here in this Edwardian postcard, was an example of his elegant design for crossing the River Severn. An identical structure (christened the Albert Edward Bridge) was used to take the Wenlock Railway across the same river at Coalbrookdale in 1864 and the design would undoubtedly have appeared at Bridgnorth if the two river crossings there proposed in the SVR's 1855 Act had not been abandoned in the Company's deviation Act of the following year. *(Commercial postcard/author's collection)*

VICTORIA BRIDGE ARLEY. 7.

**Although the SVR** was opened as, and remained, a single-track branch line, all bridges were designed and constructed to accommodate a double-track formation. This is a 2015 photograph of the surviving bridge over the Rea Brook on the outskirts of Shrewsbury. *(Author)*

at Stourport, and with John Fowler as the Company's new engineer, appointed following the death of Nicholson in November 1854, a new bill was presented to Parliament in 1855. Having reduced the projected cost from £600,000 to £480,000 and the authorised further mortgage borrowings from £200,000 to £160,000, the new route was granted Royal Assent on 30 July 1855.

Incomprehensively, barely a month later, the Company was seeking to change its plans yet again, attempting to reduce the overall mileage of the line by moving the connection with the OW&WR to the north of Hartlebury Station and by reverting to Stephenson's alignment through Bridgnorth via a tunnel. Despite what MPs and the Lords at Westminster must have thought of the

antics of Shropshire and Worcestershire railway promoters, they obligingly allowed the deviation Act to pass easily through Parliament unopposed in the summer of 1856.

But still the SVR's finances did not match its aspirations, and in 1857 another two bills were prepared, one for an extension of time to raise funds to finish the railway and the other for the complete abandonment of the project.

The delays had already weakened any lingering hopes the Company had for extracting traffic from the East Shropshire Coalfield. The S&BR's 'Coalbrookdale' branch had been operating on the eastern side of the Coalfield since 1854, and in May 1857 the W&SJR opened its branch a few miles to the west from Ketley on the GWR (S&BR) main line south

**Photographed in** March 2015 before becoming completely hidden from view by the leaves of the surrounding trees, this shows the two perfectly preserved stone arches of the double-track bridge over Cound Brook, between Berrington and Cressage stations. Unlikely to be seen by anyone other than farmers and fishermen, it illustrates the care and attention lavished by Victorian architects, civil engineers and the craftsmen, who dressed and laid the stones on modest structures like this one no matter where they were situated. *(Author)*

to Horsehay and the Coalbrookdale Company's furnaces and forges there. This line was extended two years later to connect with the S&BR's branch at Lightmoor; it too became part of the GWR in the same year. Also in 1857, the rival LNWR had obtained an Act to convert parts of the tub-boat canal into a railway as first suggested by the SUR&CC in the previous decade. This was to create a route from its Stafford line at Hadley, southwards through the heart of the Coalfield, between the other two lines, past numerous ironworks and the famous Coalport china works to a terminus directly adjacent to the existing road bridge over the Severn. This Coalport branch opened in 1861.

**Hampton Loade** Station was an example of the standard design of building used at every station on the SVR apart from Bridgnorth and Ironbridge & Broseley. Along with Cressage and Linley, it remained in its original condition when other stations of this design had additional rooms added over the years. *(Author/2001)*

It was not surprising, therefore, that in 1857 the SVR felt defeated. It toyed briefly with the idea of swinging its line over the river at Coalport to join the LNWR branch and abandoning the rest of the route to Shrewsbury, but then Morton Peto, one of the greatest railway contractors of the period, who had already invested a large amount of his own money into the project, and had also acted as the Company's chairman for many years, presented the directors with three options, one of which they could not refuse. Restricting the Company's commitment to £160,000 – the sum agreed for borrowing – his contracting company (Peto, Brassey & Betts) would accept £240,000 in shares to complete a single-track, line but with earthworks

and most other structures wide enough to accommodate two.

The abandonment bill was withdrawn, and, for the fourth time, Parliament agreed to extend the time allowed for completing yet another SVR scheme. The Royal Assent for this was secured on 23 July 1858. This time the SVR stuck to its plans, further buoyed by its recent agreement with the OW&WR, who were to maintain and run the new line for five years after completion. In late summer 1858, construction work began.

# Opening to the First World War

The line that Messrs Peto, Brassey & Betts set out to build in 1858 was very different to the double-track main line along the Severn Valley that had been envisaged in the 1840s. By the time they had finished their work it was even more modest. The only places where trains travelling in opposite directions could pass were at the stations of Buildwas, Ironbridge & Broseley, Bridgnorth, Bewdley and Stourport, and as both tunnels at Mount Pleasant (south of Bewdley) and Bridgnorth had been constructed only wide enough to take a single track, it was obvious any hope of a future double-track line had evaporated.

When work had started it was confidently predicted the railway would open in October 1860, but bad weather and landslips added another year and a quarter to the contract. During that period, the Oxford, Worcester & Wolverhampton Railway (OW&WR) had agreed to a 999-year lease of the Severn Valley Railway (SVR) within days of an amalgamation with the Newport, Abergavenny & Hereford Railway (NA&HR) and the Worcester & Hereford Railway (W&HR) to create the West Midland Railway (WMR) on 1 July 1860. This Company lasted until 1 August 1863 when it was absorbed into the Great Western Railway (GWR).

The SVR opened to the public on 1 February 1862 as part of the WMR. During the week, there were just three passenger trains in either direction using the whole route between Shrewsbury and Hartlebury, with an additional train each way between Shrewsbury and Bridgnorth. Of those, the fastest was the 10.50 from Shrewsbury that averaged 22.5 mph and reached Bewdley at 12.33, and the slowest was the 6.30 from the county town that averaged 18.5mph on its journey of six minutes short of two hours to Bewdley. Although slow compared with the speeds being attained on the country's main lines, it would have been impossible to make the same journey in a comparable time by horse-drawn vehicle on the roads between Shrewsbury and Worcester, or between any of the intermediate stations.

No matter how meagre the timetable, or how long journeys took, the opening of the SVR played a significant part in maintaining the economic viability of the communities it served. By the 1860s the emphasis was no longer on the exploitation of an area by a railway. By then, railways had become a necessary part of the healthy trading and civic life

of towns and cities, and when the SVR opened, railways were considered a means to prevent decline. The original intention of the 1840s promoters to gain access into the heart of the East Shropshire Coalfield in order to make their shareholders money may have been thwarted by 1862, but for the traders and town councillors on the route of the SVR, they were just relieved to be on the railway map at last.

Ironically, given the railway's name, the main inconvenience that remained throughout the history of the line was the River Severn. There were many locations where traders and passengers had to use either bridges or ferries to reach stations. Although within shouting distance of the town, the Station serving Ironbridge was on the opposite side of the river, it being necessary to pay a toll to use the Iron Bridge every time those from the town needed to get to and from the Station. The towns of Coalport and Bewdley were also on the opposite side of the river to their respective railway stations, although at the latter the bridge was at least free of any tolls. For those living in Hampton Loade and Arley, it was necessary to use ferries to reach the station.

**A busy scene** at Ironbridge & Broseley Station in the 1930s. A GWR 2-6-2T is at the head of a train for Bridgnorth whilst a Shrewsbury-bound train occupies the down platform. *(Author's collection)*

**Marked urgent,** this consignment note for goods sent in 1890 from Ironbridge to Llanishen on the Rhymney Railway, South Wales, was one of hundreds of thousands of such documents accompanying goods that were dispatched to and received from all parts of the country.
*(Author's collection)*

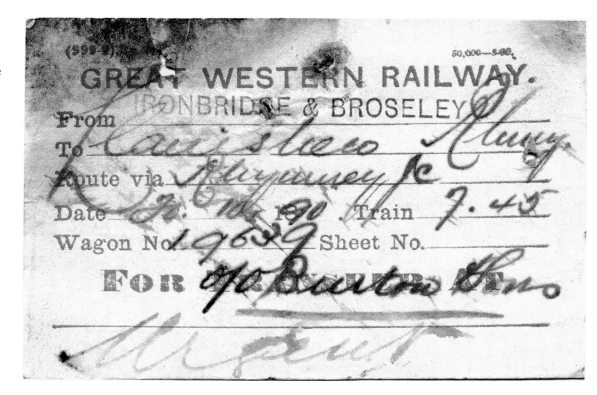

## Connecting branch lines

Of the many plans there had been since 1845 to run branch lines across the river into the Coalfield from the south, the only one that was built proved of little use to the SVR. The Company had made one last attempt to enter Coalbrookdale in 1861, only to have its plans defeated in Parliament in favour of those put forward by the Wenlock Railway (WR). This Company's scheme was essentially a continuation of the Much Wenlock & Severn Junction Railway (MW&SJR) branch already authorised to join the SVR at Buildwas. From there it was to continue across the River Severn and into Coalbrookdale. The proposal was strengthened by the GWR's commitment to extend its existing line from Lightmoor to join the WR in Coalbrookdale. The MW&SJR opened on the same day as the SVR, and then in November 1864 the

double-track route between Buildwas and Lightmoor was brought into use, with a siding into the Coalbrookdale Company's famous eighteenth-century ironworks. Significantly, a month later, the MW&SJR line was extended to limestone quarries on Wenlock Edge, and this mineral soon started to flow northwards from there, over the SVR at Buildwas, through Coalbrookdale and on to the blast furnaces in the north of the Coalfield, and further afield to the ironworks of South Staffordshire. From its opening the MW&SJR was worked by the GWR.

Two other branches made connections with the SVR, and rather than increase

**When this photograph** was taken on 23 August 1960, apart from the motive power and carriages, very little had changed at Buildwas Junction Station for decades. A train from Much Wenlock stands in the high-level platform on the left whilst below on the right, on the Severn Valley line, there is a train for Shrewsbury. *(R. Platt)*

traffic along the branch, they too tended to channel it across the railway. The first came in from the west from Tenbury, running into the north end of Bewdley Station having paralleled the SVR for a mile (1.6km) from the point where Dowles Brook joined the River Severn and where, having followed the brook through the Wyre Forest, the railway crossed the river. Built by the Tenbury & Bewdley Railway (T&BR), this line opened for passengers on 13 August 1864 as an extension to a line opened three years earlier from Woofferton Junction on the Shrewsbury & Hereford Railway (S&HR).

The second branch also ran into Bewdley, this time at the south end of the Station. This single line from Kidderminster was brought into use on

1 June 1878. Authority to build a line to connect the towns had been secured in 1861, but the powers were allowed to lapse. Another scheme was put forward in 1867 and, bundled with other GWR plans, was authorised by an Act of Parliament the following year.

By then, the S&HR and the Tenbury Railway had been taken over jointly by the GWR and the London & North Western Railway (LNWR), and the T&BR had been absorbed into the GWR's empire. Of the two companies, it was the LNWR that saw more potential in a Bewdley–Kidderminster connection than the GWR. By that short branch, the LNWR would be able to run through trains between Birmingham and the Shrewsbury–Hereford line, and perhaps beyond into the South Wales coalfield. But it was not its line to make and the LNWR was further frustrated in 1873 when the GWR tried to abandon its project in favour of an alternative new line between Stourbridge and Bewdley. This proposal did not survive the

**A view** looking towards Bewdley of Dowles Bridge that carried the Tenbury & Bewdley Railway over the River Severn. The early twentieth-century photograph was turned into a postcard, this example having been posted from Northwood (Bewdley) to Walsall on 31 May 1909. *(Commercial postcard/author's collection)*

**The north end** of Bewdley Station in 1961, the track layout unchanged since the signalbox was brought into use here in 1878. At the far end of the viaduct, the Tenbury line is on the left with the SVR line on the right. For the next mile, until they parted company near Dowles Bridge, these parallel tracks gave the appearance of double-track route, although both lines would have been used by trains travelling both north and south.
(Joe Moss via R. Carpenter)

**A late Victorian photograph** taken on Bewdley Station's island platform with its carefully-painted canopy of 1878. A society that extolled the virtues of hard physical work and cleanliness is neatly illustrated by the passengers in everyday working clothes standing in front of enamel signs advertising Hudson's Soap.
(Kidderminster Railway Museum)

Parliamentary committee stage and when the GWR still appeared reluctant to build its Bewdley–Kidderminster loop, the following year the LNWR backed an ambitious scheme to build a new line from the south of its Wolverhampton Station (High Level) to join the Tenbury line at Dowles Bridge with a short, awkward token link running through a tunnel to the north of Bewdley Station.

The project was really no more than a ploy to spur the GWR into making a start on its Bewdley–Kidderminster branch. The LNWR's tactics worked and once the 1874 Bill was defeated the GWR agreed to begin construction of its Kidderminster loop. When that finally opened, the LNWR immediately started to run a number of cross-country goods trains via Bewdley as well as through carriages between Birmingham New Street and Woofferton Junction.

## Industry

In 1862, all commercial river traffic between Coalbrookdale and Shrewsbury came to an end, and by the First World War there were no trading boats working further upstream than Arley. As outlined in the previous chapter, the river had

**An aerial view** of just part of Maw & Company's 1883 decorative tileworks at Jackfield. The SVR can be seen on the left running parallel to the eight bottle kilns in which millions of tiles were fired until the 1930s. Alongside, the sidings would have dealt with wagon load after wagon load of product dispatched to every part of the British Empire. At the top of the photograph is the huddle of houses, most of which were damaged beyond repair in the landslip of 1951. The River Severn is just out of sight to the right of the twentieth-century tennis court. (*Cambridge University Collection of Aerial Photographs/27.6.1948*)

been vital in the development of the Shropshire iron trade and although not connected, it was ironic that this industry declined in importance in the same period.

But just as the eighteenth-century ironmasters had grasped the opportunities the river offered, so a new generation of entrepreneurs looked to exploit railway communications. Despite the limitations of the number of trains that could be run over the single-track SVR line, it nevertheless offered a more reliable and convenient service than the River Severn ever had, and as it connected into an increasingly extensive national railway network, it allowed businesses to reach markets all over the country and abroad.

In 1850 John Hornby Maw took over a works in Worcester to make encaustic floor tiles recently made popular by Herbert Minton, who was manufacturing such tiles to A.W.N. Pugin's design for the new Houses of Parliament. In 1852 Maw, with his two sons and daughter, moved to a disused ironworks south of the River Severn within sight of the Iron Bridge, and set up a decorative floor and wall-tile business there. The arrival of the SVR greatly aided the distribution of their product, and they soon had clients throughout the country and the British Empire. So successful did they become that in 1883 the Maws brothers, George and Arthur, opened what was at the time the world's largest decorative tileworks at Jackfield, 1.5 miles (2.4km) east of Ironbridge, with sidings connected to the SVR. Even though Jackfield had once been described as at 'the fag end' of the world, the SVR allowed Maw & Company to compete directly with the numerous tileworks in Stoke-on-Trent, including the various Minton factories.

The man responsible for that description of Jackfield was Henry Dunnill, who, by the 1880s, was also

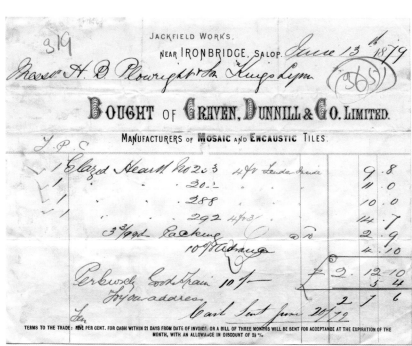

running a very successful decorative tileworks only a few hundred metres from the Maws' factory, it too gaining an international reputation. Craven Dunnill & Company had been established in 1871 and located alongside the SVR at Jackfield to take advantage of the railway. It is disappointing that, considering the number of prestigious jobs both firms secured up to the start of the First World War and the millions of tiles that would have left Jackfield on SVR trains in that period, no photographs of them appear to have survived.

Unlike Maws, Craven Dunnill & Company shared railway sidings with a number of firms in and around Jackfield and Broseley that were manufacturing bricks and roofing tiles. Although the exploitation of the excellent local clays had a long history stretching back into the sixteenth century, it was only in the early nineteenth century that the industry started to expand significantly, following the demise of iron-making immediately south of the River Severn. The river had already facilitated the widespread distribution of tiles, but the arrival

**A Craven Dunnill & Company** invoice of 1879 for hearth tiles supplied to H. B. Plowright & Son, ironmongers of Kings Lynn. These tiles, along with countless others manufactured between 1871 and the First World War, would have been dispatched in SVR trains from Jackfield Sidings. *(Author's collection)*

of the SVR considerably accelerated the industry's expansion. Broseley roofing tiles were well regarded in not just the Midlands building trade, but elsewhere in Britain and the Empire. The reputation was such that by the end of the nineteenth century manufacturers in other parts of the country were marketing 'Broseleys', forcing the Shropshire manufacturers to form an association in an attempt to safeguard 'their' name.

One of the largest local firms in this association was Exley & Sons. In 1891, it sunk a new clay mine just south-east of Coalport Station on the SVR with a connection to the railway. The Firm then established a huge new manufacturing facility on the site – Coalport Tileries –

that with all the latest machinery was capable of turning out a quarter of a million standard-sized roofing tiles a week.

Despite the use of machinery, brick and roof-tile making was predominantly a very hard manual occupation, and the industry had a reputation for the toughness of its workforce struggling in poor working conditions for little money.

Another physically-demanding industry stimulated by the opening of the SVR was coal mining. Coal had been mined around Highley before the railway was built, but in 1879 the Highley Mining Company sunk a shaft immediately west of the SVR station. In 1892, the Company sank another shaft further south on the

**By the** early years of the twentieth century, the rail connection into Highley Colliery was so often filled with wagons that the GWR was obliged to erect the footbridge seen here so that passengers from the village (to the left) were not prevented from reaching the station platform. The platform in the foreground of this photograph once supported a single-storey corrugated-tin goods shed of uncertain date. *(Joe Moss via R. Carpenter)*

Kinlet estate. It also had a connection to the SVR, a line running alongside Borle Brook to new sidings appropriately named Kinlet and brought into use in 1895 one mile (1.6km) south of Highley Station.

Eventually these sidings were shared with the Billingsley Colliery Company, when in 1913 the long-planned railway from its mine sunk in 1878 was finally completed. To cope with the increase in traffic, the ground frames at the sidings were replaced by a fully-interlocked signalbox that was bought into use in December 1913. Barely two years later, The Highley Mining Company absorbed the Billingsley Colliery Company Interestingly, coal from the Highley pits found its way to the Wilden Ironworks just outside Stourport by first running down the railway to the station yard there, then being transferred to boats in a canal basin constructed by the GWR off the Staffordshire & Worcestershire Canal in the middle of the 1880s.

**The station yard** at Stourport looking east towards Hartlebury Junction with the connection to the canal basin dropping steeply away on the left. Because this siding made a facing connection with the down running line, a trap point was provided to derail any vehicles that might accidentally be shunted past the signal (on the right) when at danger. *(R. Buckley)*

## Passengers

By the outbreak of the First World War, the GWR had made modest infrastructure improvements along the SVR benefitting both freight traffic and passengers. Highley Station was resignalled in 1883. Two new, fully-interlocked signalboxes were brought into use at Stourport at the beginning of 1886. Buildwas Station and Junction was resignalled in 1888, and provided with two new signalboxes. Another pair of signalboxes was brought into use at Bridgnorth in 1891/2. Signalling was upgraded, and loops were laid at Arley (1883), Hampton Loade (1883), Coalport (1896), Cressage (1894) and Berrington (1894), thereby increasing the capacity of

**The first** major upgrading of the signalling at Bridgnorth Station took place in 1892 when two fully-interlocked signalboxes were brought into use, the one at the south end of the Station seen here in this early twentieth-century view. With its partner, Bridgnorth North, it remained in use until a central signalbox was erected on the main platform in 1923. *(Author's collection)*

**Britain's railway network** was at its most manicured in the ten years leading up to the outbreak of the First World War. In that decade, Mr Batchelor was the station master at Arley, and in this photograph he is shown in front of just a small section of his platform flower display that consistently won prizes over many years. *(detail of GWR official)*

**The signalbox** at Cressage station was opened in July 1894 as part of the work that led to the provision of a loop and platform to serve Shrewsbury-bound (down) trains. The existing (up) platform was extended at the same time. *(R. Conway collection)*

**Berrington Station** photographed from the end of the down (Shrewsbury) platform. This platform was built in 1894 as was the loop and signalbox. In the same year improvements to increase line capacity were also carried out at Cressage and Shrewsbury. *(Lens of Sutton Association)*

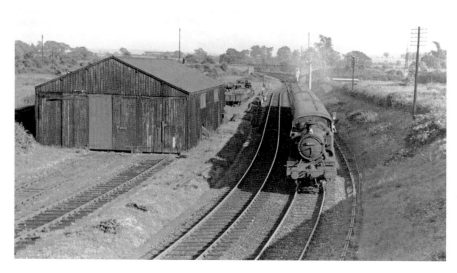

**The short section** of double-track seen here on the approach to Sutton Bridge Junction, Shrewsbury, was brought into use in 1894 with a signalbox – Burnt Mill Junction – positioned at the points that can be seen at the end of this train arriving from the south. The box closed in 1937, the points then being worked from Sutton Bridge Junction signalbox. The large timber shed on the left was for carriages. *(Author's collection)*

the line. Highley, Linley and Eardington remained the only stations where passenger trains travelling in opposite directions could not pass. Station buildings were extended at Coalport, Highley, Arley and Berrington to provide extra waiting rooms, all but the last also gaining additional first-floor bedrooms for the resident station masters. Hampton Loade, Cressage and Linley were the only station buildings of the same 'standard' design to remain unaltered. Ironbridge had never boasted upstairs rooms but an extra ground-floor room was added at the beginning of the twentieth century.

On 23 May 1898 the Kidderminster & Stourport Electric Tramway started

**One of** the new electric trams standing in the middle of Bridge Street, Stourport c1910. This photograph perfectly illustrates the convenience of a tram service running on lines simply slotted into existing streets that already formed the heart of a town, compared to a railway that was confined to its own fixed route, passengers only able to join trains at purpose-built stations. (F. Farrell/Online Transport Archive)

a service along the road connecting the two towns in its title, using, as also made clear in its title, electric trams. This provided a new and direct service far better than anything the railway could offer, as a journey between Kidderminster and Stourport by train entailed an inconvenient change either at Bewdley or at Hartlebury. The new electric tram service not only fulfilled a need, it could also boast that it was more up to date than the existing tram networks in Birmingham, Nottingham and even London, where horse-drawn services had yet to be superseded by electric traction. Where the tracks of the Kidderminster & Stourport Electric Tramway crossed those of the SVR at Stourport Station, everyone was able to compare traditional steam trains with the very latest, state-of-the-art, electric road vehicles.

As similar electric-tram services were established in other large towns

**The tracks** of the Kidderminster & Stourport Electric Tramway crossed the railway at Stourport Station level crossing until 1929 when the service ended. The 1951 extension to the former north signalbox is very obvious in this photograph. *(J. H. Moss)*

**A postcard** issued to celebrate the introduction of rail motor services between Kidderminster, Bewdley and Stourport on 2 January 1905. *(Author's collection)*

**A photograph** that has appeared before in a number of books, but one that is still worth reproducing. One of the GWR's rail motors stands closest to the footbridge having worked in from the south, whilst at the island platform is a London & North Western Railway (LNWR) through coach between Birmingham and Woofferton. The home signal in the foreground is 'off' for something to pass both trains around the west side of the island platform. *(Lens of Sutton Association)*

and cities, hundreds of people were lured away from trains, and the railway companies realised they had to respond. A number invested heavily in new equipment on various parts of their existing network, installing overhead wires to transfer current generated in their own power stations to new electric trains. Elsewhere, steam technology was refined to create new motive power, the GWR calling its variants 'rail motors'. The rail motors were a single passenger carriage incorporating a small steam engine and as they could be driven from either end, unlike traditional locomotive-hauled trains, this removed the need to

detach an engine when it had completed a journey in order to run it around its train for the return trip. The operational concept of the rail motor was exactly the same as that of multiple-unit trains in the current century.

Obviously, the GWR could not compete directly with the Kidderminster & Stourport Electric Tramway, but it must have felt it was worthwhile introducing rail motors on the southern end of the SVR because they were drafted in to run a new shuttle service between Kidderminster, Bewdley and Stourport at the beginning of January 1905. As part of this initiative, a new single-platform halt was built at Foley Park where the main Kidderminster–Stourport road, down which the tram service operated, crossed the line. Later that year another halt was opened near the rifle range on the western side of Bewdley Tunnel.

Meanwhile at Bridgnorth in the same

period, the GWR had decided to operate its own road service between the railway station there and Wolverhampton. This was introduced in 1904, the year the Company was preparing plans for a new railway link between the two towns. Since 1860, a number of schemes had been put forward, but nothing came of any of them. The new bus service started on 7 November 1904 and was operated by three Clarkston steam buses. They immediately struggled in the winter weather and although their maximum

**The original** 1905 Foley Park Halt was on the opposite side of the line to the 1925 replacement seen here. This photograph was taken looking west towards Bewdley, with the bridge taking Stourport Road (A451) across the line in the background. *(Lens of Sutton Association)*

speed did not reach double figures, they were accident-prone. In April the following year they were banished to Somerset and replaced by Milnes-Daimler buses with petrol engines. These survived in service until 1920 before being replaced with more modern vehicles.

# To Closure

### Between the wars

The period between the First and Second World Wars was an interesting one in the history of the Severn Valley branch of the Great Western Railway (GWR). In 1923 most of the railway companies in the country were grouped into four organisations – the Southern Railway (SR), the London & North Eastern Railway (LNER), the London Midland & Scottish (LMS) and the GWR. Whereas the first three were very much new creations, the GWR was in effect an enlargement of the existing Company by the addition of smaller ones, particularly in Wales. For the GWR this allowed for continuing evolution rather than revolution in the design and liveries of locomotives and carriages, in the way passengers and freight were dealt with, in signalling and countless other traditional operating practices. In many locations, nothing much seemed to change, but in others the modern world made its presence felt. A railway passenger travelling along the Severn Valley between the wars witnessed both continuity and great change.

As most railway histories relate, improved public transport on better-maintained roads throughout the country, and the rise in private-car ownership, led to a fall in the number of people using trains between the wars. On the SVR, this was most noticeable at Stourport, Bewdley, Bridgnorth and the two village stations closest to Shrewsbury: Cressage and Berrington. At all other stations, passenger numbers remained surprisingly stable although the trend was obviously one of reduced numbers. More frequent bus services that made the same inter-town connections as the railway at the extremities of the line, obviously accounted for the railway's losses there. But what is more difficult to analyse is the 66 per cent decrease in passengers using Bridgnorth Station. It may partly have been due to more people travelling to and from Wolverhampton and the Black Country rather than moving along the river valley. The GWR's various attempts to construct a railway between Bridgnorth and Wolverhampton, and the introduction of its own bus service, certainly seems to support this view. In May 1925, the GWR completed its Wombourn branch that left the line between Birmingham and Shrewsbury just north of Wolverhampton Station, running southwards to Kingswinford. Two years later it renewed powers to build a branch from Wombourn to

**Shunting cattle wagons** at the north end of Bridgnorth Station in 1934. On page 251 of the GWR's *'General Appendix to the Rule Book'* of August 1936 it stated, 'In dealing with Live Stock, including horses, cattle, sheep, pigs and goats, care and patience must be shown, not only in loading and unloading, but also in their treatment during transit, and in and about the yards, pens, sheds and stations, in order to avoid fright or injury, and consequent suffering on the part of the animals.' *(E. R. Morten)*

Bridgnorth, but the extension was never built.

If the GWR did not commit to major capital projects in the area between the wars, it did try other initiatives both to maintain passenger numbers along the valley and reduce operating costs. Just before the Grouping of 1923, the Company introduced 'auto cars' to take over the services that had been operated by the Edwardian rail motors and also to work a number of services north of Bewdley. These new trains consisted of a carriage and locomotive, which like their predecessors, could be driven from either end. From 1936, some of the GWR's very latest diesel railcars were also employed to operate between Kidderminster,

Hartlebury and Stourport, their streamlined design reflecting the spirit of a new age.

Elsewhere along the valley, the GWR opened a number of single-platform halts to encourage day-trippers and fishermen to travel on the line. The first was brought into use at the very end of March 1930 less than a mile north-west of Stourport Station and christened Burlish Halt. Others followed at Cound, 3.5 miles

**One of** the 1930s streamlined diesel railcars was still in service when photographed with a Shrewsbury-bound train at Buildwas Junction Station on 30 December 1954. The poster on the platform advertised a trip to and from the county town at 2s 2d (11p) by this train. *(R. B. Parr)*

(5.6km) south of Berrington (August 1934); Jackfield, one mile (1.6km) from Ironbridge & Broseley Station (December 1934); and Northwood, 1.5 miles (2.4km) north of Bewdley (June 1935). The halt at Foley Park that had opened in 1905 continued in use, although its partner of the same year located close to the rifle range outside Bewdley had closed in October 1920.

All railway companies between the wars realised the importance of advertising and publicity in attracting and maintaining custom. In addition to eye-catching posters, the GWR also produced a fascinating range of publications. Immediately before the start of the First World War it had published a booklet entitled *'The Severn Valley'* and

this was re-issued in the 1920s. In the following decade, to help promote the Severn Valley as a holiday destination, the GWR refurbished redundant passenger carriages as camping coaches, positioning one at Hampton Loade and the other at Arley.

By the summer of 1938, there were five through trains between Bewdley and Shrewsbury during the week (including Saturdays) with six in the opposite direction. Journeys were timetabled to take between 1 hour and 29 minutes and 1 hour and 40 minutes. There were three additional trains each way between Bewdley and Bridgnorth, with two extra trains each way between Bewdley and Highley, augmented on Saturdays by two additional trains in both directions between these stations. On Sundays there was only one train in either direction that travelled the whole length of the line, supplemented by a morning train between Shrewsbury and Bridgnorth and

**Cound Halt,** between the stations at Berrington and Cressage, was positioned immediately behind the Riverside Inn on the Shrewsbury–Cressage–Much Wenlock road (A458). It was a brisk walk from the tiny village of Cound to the east and the halt was probably of more use to fishermen, located as it was within sight of the River Severn. *(Lens of Sutton Association)*

an afternoon train between Bewdley and Bridgnorth, and then two evening trains from Bridgnorth: one to Bewdley and the other to Shrewsbury.

The service offered south of Bewdley was far more generous. Between there and Kidderminster, there were eighteen weekday trains with a number of extras on Saturdays. Some of these trains also ran between Stourport and Hartlebury to provide a service of ten trains to and from these stations during the week. In comparison the Sunday service was strangely unbalanced, with just five trains between Kidderminster and Bewdley, but nine in the opposite direction, and four between Bewdley and Stourport, none of which went on to Hartlebury, but six from Stourport to Bewdley, two of which started at Hartlebury.

The story of inter-war industry along the line is one of gains and losses, traditional 'heavy' industries suffering the most. In 1921 Billingsley Colliery

closed, followed in 1935 by the closure of Kinlet Mine and the abandonment of the lines up the Borle Brook that had served both sites. At Jackfield the two large decorative-tile works remained in production, but their output never reached the same levels as pre-war. Exley's Coalport Tileries continued in production, but the other firms manufacturing roofing tiles made less use of Jackfield Sidings, and locally-mined clay was sent to the Potteries by road.

Of the gains from industry for the railway, both financially and visually the most significant were at Kidderminster, Stourport and Buildwas. At the former, the West Midlands Sugar Company opened a large factory for the processing of locally-grown sugar beet in 1925, its sidings connected to the SVR. Production was seasonal and not always predictable, and in 1934 the Firm went into liquidation, the factory eventually

**Travelling away** from the camera, diesel railcar No. 29, forming the 4.20pm Shrewsbury to Kidderminster service on 25 June 1960, was soon to pass the remains of Kinlet Sidings just visible in the background. From there, two lines followed the Borle Brook off to the right to Kinlet and Billingsley collieries, both lines having been dismantled by the time this photograph was taken. *(Michael Mensing)*

becoming part of the British Sugar Corporation a few years later.

At Stourport and Buildwas, the landscape was considerably altered with the erection of two large electricity-generating stations. Both were located so they could take advantage of connections to the railway for the delivery of coal and were adjacent to the River Severn that provided the main water supply. Although originally planned by private companies, both stations were considered key to the strategy of the Central Electricity Board formed in 1926 to create a network of lines for supplying all parts of the country with electricity via a new National Grid. The first station to be brought on-line was at Stourport in that same year. Initially its coal supply was delivered from both the Staffordshire & Worcestershire Canal and the river, but in the first months of the Second World

War, the rail connection planned back in 1918 was brought into use. By then, the power station at Buildwas was complete (officially christened Ironbridge), the first electricity having been generated in the summer of 1932, before enlargement of the complex in 1935 and again during the winter of 1938/9. Such were the traffic demands at the site that the new **Buildwas Junction** signalbox, only opened in 1923, had to be enlarged in 1931 to accommodate a frame of 113 levers.

Ironically, although heralding a new 'electric age', the building of these power stations and others elsewhere in the country reinforced the importance of coal in the British economy. Despite the closure of Kinlet and Billingsley mines, the extraction of coal in that part of Shropshire remained important, and in 1935 a new colliery was sunk on the east

**Dominating the** background in this view taken at Buildwas Junction on 15 March 1952 is Ironbridge 'A' Power Station, still sporting its World War Two camouflage paintwork. Taking water at the head of the 3.46pm train to Much Wenlock was 0-6-0PT No. 9624, put into traffic in 1945 and still in GWR livery four years after nationalisation. *(A. Wakelin)*

**Build was** Junction looking towards Ironbridge from the Much Wenlock branch platform. The large Buildwas Junction signalbox can be seen in the middle distance, the 1931 extension (at the far end) only discernable from the rest of the 1923 signalbox by its lack of locking room windows. *(BR(W) official)*

**Two of** the three 0-4-0 saddle tanks supplied by Peckett & Sons of Bristol in 1933, 1936 and 1940 to work at Ironbridge Power Station, where this photograph was taken on 19 June 1958. *(P. Eckersley)*

side of the River Severn near Alveley. Its shafts linked in with existing seams worked by Highley Colliery, and from 1940, all coal from both sites was lifted at Alveley. Much of this was transported back across the river above ground via a new bridge to loading facilities and sidings that had been commissioned only a few months before the outbreak of war in 1939 next to the SVR, north of Highley Station.

There is no doubt all these large industrial sites boosted the fortunes of the SVR and certainly prolonged its life.

**A train** from Shrewsbury arriving at Highley Station in April 1954. Because of its rural setting, this station has become a popular location for enthusiasts and families since it passed into the hands of preservationists, and it is difficult to imagine that just out of sight on either side of the station there were collieries. *(W.A Camwell)*

**A coal train** from Alveley Colliery sidings passing through Ironbridge & Broseley Station in the final years before closure on its way to Buildwas Power Station. Once cleared of track and buildings at the end of the 1960s, this station site was turned into a car park for visitors to the Iron Bridge. (Author's collection)

But there were also a number of smaller firms that turned to the railway between the wars, helping to maintain the line's usefulness in the difficult economic climate of the times. In 1922 a siding was laid into Knowle Sands Brickworks just south of Bridgnorth. A little later, sidings were provided at the lime kilns just west of Ironbridge & Broseley Station. In 1929, within sight of Burlish Halt, sidings were laid into the Steatite & Porcelain Products Works. Amongst its products, this firm made insulators for the electrification of the LMS's former Wirral Railway's lines in 1938. Finally, in the last months before the declaration of war, a rail-connected fuel depot to be run by the Air Ministry was opened on the SVR a few miles from Hartlebury.

As was true of many other branch lines, the SVR became a vital alternative and diversionary route for trains during the Second World War. All sorts of locomotives other than GWR designs saw service on the line. Passenger trains were crowded with additional service personnel travelling to and from military bases around the Midlands, and coal trains were interspersed with freights carrying all manner of items necessary to maintain a nation at war. Just west of Stourport Station, the Ministry of Food opened a storage depot with a connection to the railway in 1941.

## The post-war years

After the war the railway returned to its familiar routines. Nationalisation in 1948 changed very little apart from the nomenclature on notice boards, timetables and tickets, and the livery of

## WORCESTER, BEWDLEY, BRIDGNORTH, BUILDWAS, and SHREWSBURY.

| Miles | Down | Week Days a.m N | a.m | a.m | a.m N | p.m | p.m N | p.m | p.m N | p.m | p.m N | p.m | Sn a.m |
|---|---|---|---|---|---|---|---|---|---|---|---|---|---|
| | (Shrub Hill) Worcester ¶ ...... dep | .. | 6 55 | 9 35 | .. | 1 15 | .. | .. | 4 56 | 5Y26 | 7 41 | .. | .. |
| 2½ | Fernhill Heath.......... | .. | 7 1 | 9 41 | .. | 1 21 | .. | .. | 5 2 | .. | .. | .. | .. |
| 5½ | Droitwich Spa.......... | .. | 7 8 | 9 47 | .. | 1 28 | .. | .. | 5 9 | 5 36 | 7 52 | .. | .. |
| 9 | Cutnall Green.......... | .. | .. | 9 54 | .. | 1 36 | .. | .. | 5 16 | .. | .. | .. | .. |
| 11½ | Hartlebury.............. | .. | 7T22 | 10L10 | .. | 2A0 | .. | .. | 5z35 | 6B10 | 8U10 | .. | .. |
| 14½ | Stourport-on-Severn ¶.. | .. | 7 33 | 10N17 | .. | 2 8 | .. | .. | 5 42 | 6 22 | 8 17 | .. | .. |
| 16¾ | Bewdley 135, 138.... arr | .. | 7 40 | 10N24 | .. | 2 15 | .. | .. | 5 49 | 6 30 | 8 24 | .. | .. |
| — | 120 Birmingham (S.H.) dep | .. | 6 12 | 8H55 | 1120 | 1P0 | 2 20 | .. | 5 0 | 5 40 | 7 10 | .. | 7 30 |
| — | 138 Kidderminster . " | 5 53 | 7 39 | 10 35 | 1240 | 2N10 | 3N30 | .. | 5 48 | 6N25 | 8 10 | .. | 8 34 |
| — | Bewdley ¶......... dep | 6 3 | 7 53 | 10 45 | 1258 | 2 24 | 3 40 | .. | 6 2 | 6 41 | 8 27 | .. | 8 46 |
| 20½ | Arley.................. | 6 16 | 8 2 | 10 55 | 1 8 | 2 33 | 3 49 | .. | 6 11 | 6 56 | 8 37 | .. | 9 0 |
| 22¾ | Highley................ | 6 22 | 8 8 | 11 2 | 1 13 | 2 39 | 3 56 | .. | 6 16 | 7 2 | 8 43 | .. | 9 8 |
| 25 | Hampton Loade ........ | .. | 8 15 | 11 9 | Saturdays only | 2 46 | 4 2 | .. | .. | 7 7 | 8 50 | .. | 9 15 |
| 27½ | Eardington ............ | .. | 8 20 | 11 15 | | 2 52 | 4 7 | .. | .. | 7 13 | Yy | .. | 9 23 |
| 29½ | Bridgnorth .... arr | .. | 8 25 | 11 19 | | 2 56 | 4 11 | .. | .. | 7 17 | 8 59 | .. | 9 27 |
| | Bridgnorth .... dep | .. | 8 28 | 11 23 | | 2 59 | .. | 5 12 | .. | 7 21 | 9 8 | .. | Not after 30th November, 1947 |
| 33¾ | Linley ................ | .. | 8 36 | 11 31 | | 3 7 | .. | 5 20 | .. | 7 29 | 9 15 | .. | |
| 36½ | Coalport H ¶ 490...... | .. | 8 41 | 11 38 | | 3 13 | .. | 5 26 | .. | 7 35 | 9 21 | .. | |
| 38½ | Iron Bridge and Broseley | .. | 8 48 | 11 54 | | 3 21 | .. | 5 34 | .. | 7 43 | 9 28 | .. | |
| 39¾ | Buildwas 133.......... | .. | 8 55 | 12 Z5 | | 3 26 | .. | 5F43 | .. | 7 48 | 9 32 | 9 40 | |
| 43¾ | Cressage ¶............ | .. | 9 2 | 12 11 | | 3 33 | .. | 5 51 | .. | 7 54 | .. | 9 46 | |
| 47¾ | Berrington..[488, 489, 492 | .. | 9 12 | 12 21 | | 3 43 | .. | 6 1 | .. | 8 4 | .. | 9 58 | |
| 52 | Shrewsbury G 108, arr | .. | 9 21 | 12 32 | .. | 3 58 | .. | 6 13 | .. | 8 17 | .. | 1017 | |

| Up | Week Days a.m N | a.m N | a.m | a.m | p.m N | p.m | p.m N | p.m | a.m N | p.m | p.m | p.m N | Sun. p.m | |
|---|---|---|---|---|---|---|---|---|---|---|---|---|---|---|
| Shrewsbury (Gen.).dep | Except Saturdays | .. | 8 15 | 11 5 | Saturdays only | 1 15 | .. | 3 30 | .. | 5 30 | 9 0 | .. | Not after 30th November, 1947 | .. |
| Berrington ¶.......... | | .. | 8 26 | 1115 | | 1 25 | .. | 3 44 | .. | 5 41 | 9 10 | .. | | .. |
| Cressage.............. | | .. | 8 37 | 1125 | | 1 35 | .. | 3 56 | .. | 5 52 | 9 20 | .. | | .. |
| Buildwas 133.......... | | .. | 8V59 | 1135 | | 1K50 | .. | 4 5 | .. | 6 3 | 9 28 | 9 38 | | .. |
| Iron Bridge & Broseley ¶ | | .. | 9 7 | 1147 | | 1 56 | .. | 4 11 | .. | 6 9 | .. | 9 43 | | .. |
| Coalport H 490........ | | .. | 9 15 | 1154 | | 2 4 | .. | 4 19 | .. | 6 16 | .. | 9 50 | | .. |
| Linley ................ | | .. | 9 21 | 12 1 | | 2 11 | .. | 4 25 | .. | 6 22 | .. | 9 56 | | .. |
| Bridgnorth ....... arr | | .. | 9 29 | 12 8 | | 2 18 | .. | 4 35 | .. | 6 29 | .. | 10 3 | | .. |
| Bridgnorth ....... dep | | .. | 9 34 | 1214 | | 3 5 | 4 20 | .. | .. | 6 33 | .. | 10 5 | 6 15 | .. |
| Eardington ............ | | .. | 9 39 | 1219 | | 3 10 | 4 25 | .. | .. | 6 38 | .. | Zz | 6 23 | .. |
| Hampton Loade......... | | .. | 9 44 | 1225 | | 3 15 | 4 31 | .. | .. | 6 43 | .. | 1015 | 6 30 | .. |
| Highley................ | 6 7 | 7 12 | 9 51 | 1234 | 1 25 | 3 23 | 4 39 | .. | 6 20 | 6 48 | .. | 1023 | 6 37 | .. |
| Arley ¶................ | 6 13 | 7 17 | 9 57 | 1241 | 1 31 | 3 29 | 4 46 | .. | 6 26 | 6 58 | .. | 1029 | 6 45 | .. |
| Bewdley 135, 138... arr | 6 21 | 7 25 | 10 5 | 1252 | 1 39 | 3 37 | 4 54 | .. | 6 34 | 7 6 | .. | 1037 | 6 54 | .. |
| 139 Kidderminster.. arr | .. | 7 39 | 1018 | 1N11 | 1 52 | 3 49 | 5 6 | .. | .. | 7 16 | .. | .. | 7 8 | .. |
| 118 Birmingham (S.H.) " | .. | 8 41 | 1136 | 2 35 | 3 31 | 5 14 | 6 35 | .. | .. | 9 15 | .. | .. | 8 26 | .. |
| Bewdley ¶.......... dep | 6 40 | 7 40 | .. | 1 0 | .. | .. | .. | .. | .. | 7 12 | .. | 1038 | .. | .. |
| Stourport-on-Severn.... | 6 48 | 7 50 | .. | 1 10 | .. | .. | .. | .. | .. | 7 20 | .. | 1046 | .. | .. |
| Hartlebury 118.......... | 6O54 | 7R57 | .. | 1G17 | .. | .. | .. | .. | .. | 7J27 | .. | 1053 | .. | .. |
| Cutnall Green.......... | .. | 8 15 | .. | .. | .. | .. | .. | .. | .. | .. | .. | .. | .. | .. |
| Droitwich Spa 660...... | 7 39 | 8 24 | .. | 1 45 | .. | .. | .. | .. | .. | 8 17 | .. | 11 5 | .. | .. |
| Fernhill H'th ¶656.. | 7 44 | 8 30 | .. | .. | .. | .. | .. | .. | .. | 8 23 | .. | .. | .. | .. |
| Worcester F 117, 122 arr | 7Y53 | 8 35 | .. | 1 55 | .. | .. | .. | .. | .. | 8 32 | .. | 1115 | .. | .. |

A Arr. 1 44 p.m B Arr. 5 25 p.m C Dep. 1 33 p.m F Shrub Hill. F Arr. 5 38 p.m G General. H About 200 yards to L.M. & S. Station.
H Dep. 9 45 a.m on Sats. J Dep. 8 6 p.m K Arr. 1 43 p.m L Arr. 10 0 a.m Third class only. Limited accommodation.
N or N Third class only Limited accommodation. O Dep. 7 29 a.m P Dep. 1 3 pm on Sats. R Dep. 8 10 a.m.
T Arr. 7 17 a.m U Arr. 8 3 p.m V Arr 8 43 a.m Y Foregate St. Station Yy Stops to set down on notice to Guard at Hampton Loade.
Z Arr. 11 ?8 a.m Zz Stops to set down on notice to Guard at Bridgnorth. z Arr. 5 25 p.m
¶ "Halts" at Astwood between Worcester (S.H.) and Fernhill Heath; at Burlish, between Stourport-on-Severn and Bewdley; at Northwood between Bewdley and Arley; at Jackfield, between Coalport and Iron Bridge and Broseley; and at Cound, between Cressage and Berrington.

**LOCAL TRAINS** between Worcester and Hartlebury, page 118—Hartlebury and Bewdley 138.

**OTHER TRAINS** between Worcester and Droitwich, page 660

**Great Western Railway** timetable, October 1947, from *'Bradshaw's Guide'. (Author's collection)*

## KIDDERMINSTER, STOURPORT-ON-SEVERN, and HARTLEBURY

| Miles | Up | Week Days a.m | | | | | | | | | | | | | | | | | | | | | | | | | | | | | | | p.m | | Sundays a.m | | | | |
|---|---|---|---|---|---|---|---|---|---|---|---|---|---|---|---|---|---|---|---|---|---|---|---|---|---|---|---|---|---|---|---|---|---|---|---|---|---|---|---|
| | | N | | N | | | N | | | N | | | N | | N | S | | | S | E | N | Z | N | | | | | N | N | | N | | | N | | | | | |
| | HOUR ☞ | 5 | | 6 | | 7 | 7 | 7 | | 8 | 8 | | 10 | 10 | 11 | 12 | | 1 | 1 | 1 | 2 | 2 | 3 | | 4 | 4 | | 5 | 6 | | 7 | 8 | | 10 | | 8 | 9 | | |
| | | | | | | | | | | | | | | | | N | | | | N | | | | | | | | | | | | | | Y | | J | V | | |
| — | Kidderminster ¶ . dep. | 53 | . | . | . | 0 | . | 39 | . | . | 50 | . | 18 | 35 | . | 40 | . | . | 31 | 45 | 10 | . | 30 | . | . | 38 | . | 48 | 25 | . | . | 10 | . | . | . | 34 | 8 | . | . |
| 3½ | Bewdley ¶ 136.... arr | 2 | . | . | . | 9 | . | 48 | . | . | 59 | . | 27 | 44 | . | 50 | . | . | 39 | 54 | 19 | . | 39 | . | . | 47 | . | 58 | 35 | . | . | 19 | . | . | . | 42 | 16 | . | . |
| | Bewdley dep | . | . | 40 | . | . | 40 | . | . | 40 | . | . | . | . | 10 | . | . | 0 | . | . | . | 25 | . | . | 42 | . | . | . | . | . | 12 | 28 | . | 38 | . | V | 24 | . | . |
| 6 | Stourport-on-Severn .... | . | . | 48 | . | . | 50 | . | . | 49 | . | . | . | . | 19 | . | . | 10 | . | . | . | 33 | . | . | 50 | . | . | . | . | . | 20 | 36 | . | 46 | . | . | 30 | . | . |
| 9 | Hartlebury........ arr | . | . | 54 | . | . | 57 | . | . | 55 | . | . | . | . | 26 | . | . | 17 | . | . | . | 40 | . | . | 56 | . | . | . | . | . | 27 | 43 | . | 53 | . | . | . | . | . |

A Stops to set down on informing Guard at Rushbury E Except Sats. H From and to Birmingham, page 139. First & Third class. J Not after 30th November. N Third class only, limited accommodation. P Craven Arms and Stokesay. S Sats only. U Third class only daily and limited accommodation on Sats. V Does not call at the Halts. W Except Sats. and does not call at the Halts. Y Stops at Burlish Halt to set down on informing Guard at Bewdley, Z Mons. to Fris.. 3rd class only, limited accommodation. First and third class Saturdays only. 3 Third class only,

## HARTLEBURY, STOURPORT-ON-SEVERN, and KIDDERMINSTER

| Miles | Down | Week Days a.m | | | | | | | | | | | | | | | | | | | | | | | | | | | | | | | | p.m | Sundays a.m | | p.m | | |
|---|---|---|---|---|---|---|---|---|---|---|---|---|---|---|---|---|---|---|---|---|---|---|---|---|---|---|---|---|---|---|---|---|---|---|---|---|---|---|---|
| | | | | | | | | N | | N | | | N | | N | | N | S | | | | | | | N | N | | N | N | | | | N | | | | | | | |
| | HOUR ☞ | 6 | | 7 | 7 | | 8 | 8 | | 9 | | 10 | 10 | 11 | 11 | | 1 | 1 | | 2 | | 3 | 4 | | 4 | 4 | | 5 | 6 | 6 | 7 | | 8 | 8 | | | 10 | | 6 | 6 | |
| | | | | | | | | | | | | | | | | | | N | | | | | | | | | | | | | | | | | | | V | | V | J | |
| — | Hartlebury ........ dep | . | . | . | 22 | . | . | 16 | . | . | . | . | 10 | . | 55 | . | . | . | . | 0 | . | . | 0 | . | . | . | . | 35 | . | 10 | . | . | 10 | . | . | . | . | . | 5 | . | . |
| 3 | Stourport-on-Severn ¶.. | . | . | . | 33 | . | . | 23 | . | . | . | . | 17 | . | 2 | . | . | . | . | 8 | . | . | 7 | . | . | . | . | 42 | . | 22 | . | . | 17 | . | . | . | 5 | . | 14 | . | . |
| 5½ | Bewdley ¶........ arr | . | . | . | 40 | . | . | 30 | . | . | . | . | 24 | . | 9 | . | . | . | . | 15 | . | . | 14 | . | . | . | . | 49 | . | 30 | . | . | 24 | . | . | . | 11 | . | 20 | . | . |
| | Bewdley dep | 3 | . | 30 | . | . | 0 | . | . | 0 | . | 9 | . | 3 | 20 | . | 2 | 42 | . | . | . | 40 | . | . | 48 | 57 | . | . | 0 | . | 7 | . | . | 46 | . | . | 21 | . | 30 | 58 | . |
| 9 | Kidderminster 135 arr | 12 | . | 39 | . | . | 9 | . | . | 10 | . | 18 | . | 12 | 29 | . | 11 | 52 | . | . | . | 49 | . | . | 57 | 6 | . | . | 10 | . | 16 | . | . | 59 | . | . | 29 | . | 38 | 8 | . |

A Stops at 5 9 p.m to take up D Stops 5 49 p.m to take up E or E Except Sats F Handsworth & Smethwick H Oldbury and Langley Green J Not after 30th November N Third class only. Limited accommodation. S or S Sats, only V Not calling at the Halts X Stops to set down from Malvern (Great) and beyond on notice to the Guard at Malvern (Great) 3 Third class only. ¶ "Halts" at Burlish, between Stourport-on-Severn and Bewdley; and at Foley Park, between Bewdley and Kidderminster.

**OTHER TRAINS** between Hartlebury and Kidderminster, see page 118

Where the MINUTES under the Hours change to a LOWER figure and DARKER type it indicates the NEXT HOUR

**Great Western Railway** timetable, October 1947, from *'Bradshaw's Guide'. (Author's collection)*

One of the former GWR's diesel railcars at Arley with a Shrewsbury–Hartlebury service on 16 April 1953. The only change since the 1930s that would have reminded passengers that the railway was no longer run by the GWR was the new livery of the railcar: chocolate and cream having been replaced by red and cream. *(W. A. Camwell)*

A south-bound train hauled by ex-GWR 2-6-2T No. 5538 waiting at Bridgnorth Station on 22 August 1961. The engine had been allocated to Shrewsbury Shed the previous month and survived only another few months before withdrawal for scrapping. The corrugated-metal shed to the side of the locomotive once housed the bus that operated the GWR's Bridgnorth–Wolverhampton service. *(H. B. Priestley)*

**Ex-GWR 0-6-0** No. 3214 heading southwards with a mixed-freight train past the ruins of Buildwas Abbey sometime in the 1950s. *(Author's collection)*

**An ex-GWR 0-6-0** pannier tank shunting at Bewdley in the 1950s. Railway work such as this had not changed in 100 years, whereas the way goods could be handled on the country's roads in the same period had been transformed beyond recognition with the introduction of diesel-engined lorries. *(Author's collection)*

locomotives and carriages. Along with other former GWR lines, the Severn Valley branch became part of British Railways, Western Region. Steam-hauled trains continued to run the passenger and freight services, with a new generation of diesel railcars joining the GWR inter-war vehicles. The railway continued to do what it had been designed to do whilst gradually, as the standard of living improved, families took control of their own transport needs by buying a car, and industry turned to a new generation of more powerful diesel-engined lorries that could dispatch and deliver door-to-door.

It soon became clear to everyone that branch lines were struggling and that was very obvious on the SVR. In 1951

**Shunting at** Bridgnorth on 25 May 1961 with ex-GWR 2-6-2T No. 6128, shedded at Kidderminster at the time. Freight traffic would continue to be handled at the station for another two and a half years until the end of 1963. *(R. G. Nelson via Terry Walsh)*

Knowle Sands Sidings were taken out of use. The following year there was a major landslip at Jackfield that destroyed many houses and dragged the railway 25ft (7.6m) closer to the river. The line was soon reinstated, but the re-located Jackfield Halt did not reopen until March 1954. By then the area and its industries were in terminal decline. The signalbox at Ironbridge & Broseley Station closed in 1956 and two years later Jackfield Sidings were taken out of use. Further south, the sidings serving Maw & Company's

**According to** the information written on the back of this photograph, this view of Ironbridge & Broseley Station and signalbox was taken on 19 July 1941, making it the product of a very risky 'snap' in wartime. During the conflict, the signalmen here would have been kept busy with additional traffic, but after the war, the signalbox only remained in use for a further eleven years. *(R. E. Lusten)*

**A view** of Coalport Station looking westwards towards Ironbridge photographed from the up starting signal worked from lever No. 29 in Coalport signalbox. The scene of quiet neglect was typical of branch-line stations in their final years of British Railways ownership. *(Author's collection)*

**A Shrewsbury arrival** at Bewdley Station in the 1950s. Despite the time-honoured routines of operating a steam-worked railway that continued in this decade, new locomotives did find their way onto the Severn Valley branch. British Railways Standard Class 3 2-6-2T No. 82008, seen here, was built in 1952 and spent most of its time working from the motive power depots (MPDs) at Kidderminster and Worcester before ending up at Taunton in 1961. *(R. J. Buckley)*

**Another British Railways** Class 3 2-6-2T that worked very briefly along the Severn Valley was No. 82005, seen here leaving Bewdley with the 4.35pm for Shrewsbury on 29 April 1961. It had only just been transferred from Chester to Shrewsbury MPD, but was quickly moved again from there to Machynlleth in July that year. *(David Johnson)*

**Diesel railcars** and British Railways' diesel multiple units (DMUs), as seen here at Bewdley Station, did help maintain passenger numbers on many branch-line services in the late 1950s. The number of passengers in this photograph gives an indication as to why trains continued to run to and from Bewdley, Hartlebury and Kidderminster on the Birmingham–Droitwich Spa line until 1969, three years after the rest of the Severn Valley line had closed. *(Author's collection)*

**Disappearing away** from Buildwas Junction to Much Wenlock in its final years of operation is what had become known to locals as 'The Dodger'. The large water tower was a legacy of the time when the engines of long mineral trains to the limestone quarries along Wenlock Edge had to fill their tanks ready for the challenging 1 in 42 climb through Farley Dingle to Much Wenlock. *(Author's collection)*

decorative tileworks were closed in 1959, and the Factory itself ended production ten years later. The connection at Coalport Station to the former Exley's roofing-tile works was severed in 1957 shortly after tile production there ceased.

For branch lines like the SVR there seemed very little British Railways could do to stop the haemorrhage of people and goods. The use of diesel railcars and diesel multiple units (DMUs) had helped, but the only other strategy appeared to be a reduction of services. In July 1961 regular passenger trains stopped running between Bewdley and Tenbury, although an experimental schools service continued for another year. In that same month (July 1962), passengers could no longer travel from Wellington, through Coalbrookdale to Buildwas Junction and Much Wenlock.

This was just a month following British Railways' announcement of its intention to withdraw passenger and freight services along the SVR between Shrewsbury and Bewdley, at the same time rationalising the services south from

**A small consignment** is unloaded from a Shrewsbury-bound ex-GWR diesel railcar at Hampton Loade Station on 16 April 1954. This sort of untroubled rural railway idyll was considered an anathema when Ernest Marples became Minister of Transport five years later, and by the time he left office in 1964, his protégé, Richard Beeching, had successfully eradicated such scenes from most of the British Railways' network. *(R. K. Blencowe Photo Archive)*

**Ex-GWR 2-6-2T**
No. 4147 taking water at the north end of Bridgnorth Station in the early 1960s. The locomotive was allocated to Kidderminster MPD in April 1961, the cast shed plate marked 84C at the bottom of the smokebox door confirming its home. *(Kidderminster Railway Museum)*

**A deserted** Highley Station in the late 1950s. *(Lens of Sutton Association)*

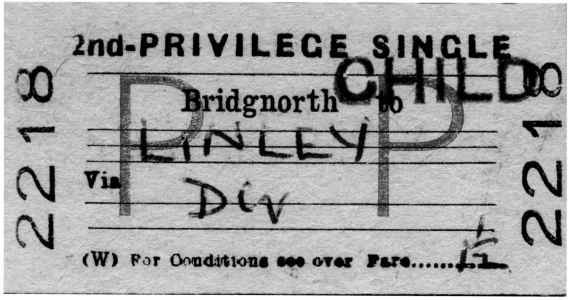

2nd-PRIVILEGE SINGLE

Bridgnorth to CHILD

LINLEY

Via DIV

(W) For Conditions see over Fare......

2218

**Bridgnorth–Linley ticket.** *(P. Waller collection)*

**Buildwas Junction Station** photographed on 18 May 1961, a scene that would be radically changed only three years later with the erection of Ironbridge 'B' Electricity Generating Power Station. The course of the SVR tracks to the left would become sidings for the new power station, whilst the rest of the station buildings, platforms and water tower were bulldozed away. *(R. G. Nelson via Terry Walsh)*

there. This was nine months before the publication of the *'Beeching Report'* that simply incorporated the recommendation with all its other closure plans. Objections were made, considered and rejected, and on 9 September 1963 the line north of Bewdley was closed to passengers, with freight and parcels traffic ending at the close of the year.

In the spring of 1964, the site of Buildwas Junction Station was cleared for the construction of a new electricity generating station (which was designated Ironbridge 'B'), and with the erection of one of its four huge cooling towers on the trackbed of the SVR, as a through route the line was physically and symbolically severed. All coal deliveries were then made via the line through Coalbrookdale.

Paradoxically, considering this development and the losses listed above, it was industry that kept the section of the line operational north of Bewdley after the passenger trains had been withdrawn. Coal trains continued to and from Alveley Sidings until the end of March 1969, by which time preservationists were in a strong position to confidently negotiate with British Railways for an extension of their line from Hampton Loade to Bewdley. The continuing use by British Railways of the line between Kidderminster Junction and the British Sugar Corporation's factory also helped the preservationists reach Kidderminster in 1984, but that is a story for the next chapter.

The sidings that had once served the Steatite & Porcelain Products Works were taken out of use in 1966 and then on 5 January 1970, British Railways' passenger services south of Bewdley finally came to an end with the closure of Stourport Station and Burlish Halt, and the withdrawal of passenger trains to and from Kidderminster. Almost exactly

a year later, the railway connection to Stourport Power Station was closed, followed in 1984 by the decommissioning and demolition of the Station itself. The future of what remained of the Severn Valley branch of the GWR was then firmly in the preservationists' hands of the Severn Valley Railway Company Ltd and its support organisations.

**Coal from** Alveley Colliery making its way southwards through Bewdley Station on a sunny 29 June 1966, the train pulled by former London, Midland & Scottish (LMS) Class 8F 2-8-0 No. 48531, shedded at the time at Oxley MPD, Wolverhampton. *(Roger Siviter)*

# Preservation

After British Railways closed the Severn Valley Railway (SVR) as a through route, it continued to run passenger trains to Bewdley from both Hartlebury and Kidderminster, and coal trains to and from Alveley Colliery Sidings. It also retained a short section of line in Shrewsbury linking Sutton Bridge Junction to sidings serving an oil depot at the former Shropshire & Montgomery Railway (S&MR) terminus opposite Shrewsbury Abbey. Surprisingly, this and the railway connection remained in use until 1988. Southwards to Buildwas, the line was officially closed at the end of January 1968 after being used to deliver equipment to the power station. Beyond the power station, through Ironbridge & Broseley Station, through Jackfield, Coalport and onwards towards Bridgnorth, track removal had started in 1964. Just north of the station there, work stopped, giving enthusiasts

**Berrington Station** as it appeared on 8 April 1965, the tracks through the down platform left *in situ* for trains delivering parts for the new Ironbridge 'B' Power Station, 7 miles (11km) away in the distance. Only three months later, 33 miles (53km) away in Kidderminster, plans were being formulated to save the SVR south from Bridgnorth for very different reasons. *(R. G. Nelson via Terry Walsh)*

just enough time to form a society for the preservation of what remained southwards to Alveley Colliery Sidings.

Timing has always been important in railway preservation. The wide-scale resentment of the closure of lines and stations brought about by the *Beeching Report* of 1963 fuelled not just an interest and nostalgia for old railways and steam engines, but also encouraged an active involvement in preservation. The 1960s was the decade of rebellion against the establishment, the era of the teenager, of weird and colourful fashion, pop music and 'dropping out', and, ironically, this challenging of the rules also empowered those who wanted to preserve the more traditional things the establishment

**Two recently-preserved** former GWR locomotives – 2-6-2T No. 4555 leading 0-4-4T No. 1420 – passing through the remains of Arley Station en route to Alveley Colliery Sidings during the afternoon of 19 September 1965. The special had been organised by the Stephenson Locomotive Society (SLS) as part of a round trip to and from Worcester Shrub Hill, returning via Wolverhampton Low Level Station. *(R. C. Riley)*

wanted to jettison. There was huge popular public support for determined groups of enthusiasts in various parts of the country who planned to run the lines British Railways no longer wanted. It was a case of 'steam power to the people'.

On 6 July 1965, at a meeting in the *Cooper's Arms*, Kidderminster, the Severn Valley Railway Society (SVRS) was created. Contact was made with British Railways and negotiations for

**British Railways** 2-6-0 No. 43106 (built in 1951 to an LMS design of 1947) arrived at Bridgnorth in fully working order in August 1968 and hauled passenger trains on the official opening of the preserved SVRC in May 1970. It is seen here just south of the Station shortly before work started on the bypass bridge at the end of 1982. At the time of writing, 'The Flying Pig' as it is nicknamed, remains in regular service on the SVR. *(Author)*

purchase entered into for everything that survived between Bridgnorth and Hampton Loade, including land, track and structures. The timing of this liaison was again important as it prevented any further track from being lifted at Bridgnorth, although it came too late to save the signalbox and signals. At the very beginning of February 1966, a purchase price of £25,000 was agreed with British Railways. Fund-raising began, aided by a number of open days

at Bridgnorth during the summer, which allowed the Society to hand over a 10 per cent deposit in February the following year. Then on 1 May 1967 the Severn Valley Railway Company Ltd (SVRC) was formed to complete the purchase.

The next step was to secure a Light Railway Order (LRO) that would allow the preservationists to operate passenger trains between Bridgnorth and Hampton Loade. British Railways would make the application and then transfer the LRO to the SVRC. But two other establishment bodies immediately tested the resolve of the new organisation. It was already known that Shropshire County Council had plans to construct a bypass road to the south of Bridgnorth. If the LRO was granted, that would oblige the Council to construct a bridge to carry the railway over the new road, a financial commitment it was not prepared to make. Consequently, the Council tabled its opposition to the granting of an LRO. The second challenge arose at the end of the year when British Coal announced the closure of the collieries at Highley and Alveley. This would immediately make the line southwards to Bewdley redundant, and if British Railways was not to recover the tracks, even more money would be needed to purchase that section. Within months of this announcement, British Railways confirmed the withdrawal of all passenger services south of Bewdley as

from April 1969. The question was then, was the SVRC in a position to buy the whole 12.5 mile (20km) route between Bridgnorth and Bewdley, secure a LRO and run its own trains?

Following a two-day public enquiry at the beginning of October 1968, objections to the granting of the LRO were dismissed, but the Minister of Transport overturned the decision. In March 1969 Alveley Colliery Sidings closed and the

**British Railways** 2-6-4T No. 80079, seen here at Bridgnorth in the 1980s, was another of the first generation of preserved locomotives, arriving on the SVR in 1971. By then Bridgnorth had become the base for the SVR's growing fleet of locomotives. The preparation of engines for their daily work, along with repairs and maintenance, was mostly carried out in the open, save for a few tasks undertaken in the former goods shed. Working conditions were improved in 1978, when the structure shown here was erected. *(Author)*

**The first stretch** of the reopened SVR, between Bridgnorth and Hampton Loade, involved trains tackling rising gradients to Eardington Summit, just beyond the short Knowle Sands Tunnel (officially an over-bridge) seen here in May 1986. The emerging locomotive is former GWR 4-6-0 No. 4930 *Hagley Hall*, built at Swindon in 1929 and purchased by the SVRHC in June 1972. *(Author)*

line between there and Bewdley went out of use.

The history of the Severn Valley Railway could have ended there. Preservation success was, and is, not guaranteed. Following closure of the former Great Western Railway (GWR) branch from Totnes to Ashburton in Devon, a group of businessmen had formed the Dart Valley Light Railway Ltd to preserve the line and in April 1969 the picturesque terminus at Ashburton was re-opened. This renaissance, however, was short-lived because the preservationists were unable to prevent the County Council from making improvements to the A38 road at Buckfastleigh in 1971 that severed

the railway and isolated the terminus from the rest of the branch. In 1969 many SVRC members and supporters would have been aware of the threat the upgrading of the A38 posed to Ashburton Station and must have felt the same fears for the Station at Bridgnorth.

Their anxiety was reduced a little following negotiations with Shropshire County Council during the summer of 1969, when it was agreed the SVRC

**From Eardington Summit**, the line drops down to Eardington Halt, approximately 2.5 miles (4km) from Bridgnorth, through the sandstone cutting seen here. This southbound train photographed in 1985 was hauled by British Railways Standard Class 4MT 2-6-0 No. 75069, an engine that came to the SVR from Barry Scrapyard in 1973. After a long period of restoration it returned to traffic in 1984 and was to continue to work trains for a further ten years until withdrawn for another major overhaul. *(Author)*

**In September 1971**, the SVR took delivery of 2-10-0 *Gordon*, then owned by The Transport Trust, who had acquired the locomotive when it was made redundant with the closure of the Longmoor Military Railway. Despite its obviously non-branch line size and livery, it worked for many years on the SVR, and was photographed here on 30 August 1982, backing into Bridgnorth Station. Catching the sun in the background is the tower of Thomas Telford's St Mary's Church. *(Author)*

would finance the bypass bridge in return for the Council withdrawing its objection to the LRO. But with money still being raised to complete the purchase of the line to Hampton Loade, and with acquisition of the rest of the line still in the balance, it remained a real possibility that Bridgnorth Station would be lost if sufficient funds could not be raised in the near future.

Objections had delayed the withdrawal of British Railways' passenger service to

**A popular** locomotive that started working on the SVR at the very end of the 1970s was former GWR 4-6-0, No. 7812 *Erlestoke Manor*, seen here entering Hampton Loade Station from the north on 5 September 1982. The engine is owned by the Erlestoke Manor Fund, as is sister locomotive No. 7802 *Bradley Manor*, which re-entered traffic in 1993, joining No. 7819 *Hinton Manor* of the same class that had been acquired by another group with SVRHC support in 1973. *(Author)*

**As well as** an impressive stud of main-line locomotives, the SVR soon became renowned for its fleet of historic carriages. Over the years complete trains of authentic GWR, LNER, LMS and BR stock have been restored at Bewdley. In this view at Little Rock just south of Eardington, former LMS 4-6-0 No. 5690 *Leander* is seen with a matching rake of seven LMS carriages. *(Adrian White)*

and from Bewdley, although it ceased to run from 5 January 1970, just a few weeks after the SVRS and SVRC were merged. In March the Minister of Railways' inspector visited Bridgnorth, declared the railway fit for the carriage of paying passengers and the LRO was transferred from British Railways to the SVRC. It had been almost exactly three years since the first preserved steam locomotive – GWR 0-6-0 No. 3205 – had been put to work at

Bridgnorth on 25 March 1967 and it was this locomotive that operated the SVRC's first regular weekend timetable from 23 May 1970. It was a triumphant moment.

Then, just as the visitors began to flock to Bridgnorth to enjoy a trip behind a steam engine, services had to be suspended. Someone in British Railways' legal department had realised that as full payment for the line had not yet been received from the SVRC, it was still technically owned by the British Railways Board and, therefore, was subject to the ban of running steam engines on the national rail network, excepting *Flying Scotsman*! The requisite funds were quickly raised, handed over to British Railways on 24 June and steam trains began running again three days later.

In February 1971, British Railways and the SVRC agreed a purchase price of £74,000 for the line south from

**This view** of Arley Station in patriotic mood taken in June 2002, belies the hard work carried out in the early 1970s to restore platforms, track and the signalling here. The work of all the volunteers who had transformed the site from its derelict state was rewarded in 1983 when the Station won the Association of Railway Preservation Societies and Ian Allan Publishing award for Best Restored Station of the Year. Many other accolades were to follow. *(Author)*

Alveley, through Bewdley to just east of Foley Park Halt, this figure including the land, track, structures and all the equipment that remained *in situ*. To raise this amount, the-then MP for South Worcestershire, Sir Gerald Nabarro, suggested the formation of the Severn Valley Railway (Holdings) Company (SVRHC) that would launch a share issue. The new organisation, with Nabarro as Chairman, then became the railway's owner, with the existing SVRC responsible for operating the line. Not all members supported this more 'commercial' development, and yet another organisation was formed – the Severn Valley Railway Association (SVRA) – to 'safeguard the interests of the members of the SVRC'.

The SVRHC share issue was launched in April 1972 and quickly reached its target, enabling the line to Foley Park to be purchased. Over the Easter holiday period, 6,400 passengers were carried between Bridgnorth and Hampton Loade, and throughout the year, restoration and maintenance of locomotives and carriages enabled a professional and successful train service to be operated using ten steam engines. Everywhere improvements were being made, with work on the rebuilt signalboxes at Bridgnorth and Hampton Loade that had started back in 1968 nearing completion, and volunteers at Arley Station optimistically tidying the platforms and the remaining single track.

In March 1973, after a difficult few months, Sir Gerald Nabarro resigned as Chairman of the SVRHC (he died in November). At the time the issue of the railway's northern terminus was still unresolved, and with work on the new bypass planned for 1975, there remained

**The 'pole route'** at Arley, a once familiar sight at the side of every railway line in the country. These rows of poles supporting a web of telegraph wires maintained communication between signalboxes and stations. In the early days of preservation, some wanted them removed, believing they spoiled photographs of trains. Then there was a period when SVR pole routes were activity restored and maintained, but in the twenty-first century with increasingly stringent regulations about 'working at height', they are once again being removed, to be replaced by cables at ground level. *(Author)*

**Erlestoke Manor** on Borle Brook Viaduct in April 1984 carefully negotiating a section of original GWR track, made up of bullhead rail, supported in cast chairs secured to timber sleepers set in ash ballast. Locomotives, and to a certain extent carriages, are the focus of most visitors' attention during their journeys along the SVR, but a vital task not always appreciated by the public is the maintenance and periodic replacement of track. *(Author)*

the possibility the SVRHC might sell the Bridgnorth station site to raise capital and to save the costs of building the bridge, forcing operations to be cut back to Eardington, 2 miles (3.5km) further south. However, this option was resoundingly rejected at a well-attended extraordinary general meeting of the SVRC held on 18 May.

This decision injected a more positive spirit amongst the members of all the organisations involved with the railway and much was achieved in 1973. Hampton Loade signalbox was commissioned in May and by the end of

the year there were 27 steam locomotives on the line, including British Railways' first Standard class passenger locomotive, 4-6-2 *Britannia*, and the War Department's imposing 2-10-0, *Gordon*. Not all the engines were operational, but it was nevertheless an impressive line-up for visitors.

In February 1973, BR was granted a

**A busy day** at Highley on 21 April 1985. Careful repair and maintenance work by a dedicated team of volunteers, led by a volunteer station master with an eye for detail, earned Highley the Best Preserved Station Award in 1982. The same sort of meticulous work by a 'rival' team at Arley was rewarded the following year. *(Author)*

**Former GWR** pannier tank No. 5764 heading a northbound train on recently-relaid track at the site of the long-closed miners' halt just north of Highley. This locomotive was another of the SVR's 1970s fleet, delivered in full working order from London Transport in June 1971. *(Author)*

**Former GWR** 2-8-0 No. 2857, completed at Swindon Works in 1918, was rescued by 'The 2857 Society' in 1974 and moved to the SVR for restoration. Seen here at Highley on a misty 28 September 1985 morning, it is at the head of a mixed-goods train, all the wagons of which had also been restored by enthusiasts over a number of years. *(Author)*

**Former LMS** 2-6-0 No. 46443 was the second steam engine to be brought to the SVR, arriving on 22 April 1967. It had been purchased privately in working order from BR and was bought by the SVRHC in 1972. In 1983, controversy was sparked when the locomotive was sold, but such was the support for what became known as 'The People's Engine', money was quickly raised by the 'SVR 46443 Fund' whose purchase ensured the engine could continue to work on the line. It was photographed with 2-6-0 No. 43106 approaching Bewdley from the north on 21 September 1986. *(Author)*

**When this photograph** was taken of former LMS 4-6-0 No. 5690 *Leander* crossing Borle Brook Viaduct, and heading for Arley and Bewdley on 22 April 1984, the locomotive had only just been purchased by the SVRHC. After five years out of action awaiting restoration, the locomotive was sold in 1994, the sale which was to have involved 2-6-0 No. 46443 as well. Unlike the latter engine, *Leander* did leave the railway, only returning briefly in 2010 for the 40th anniversary of the re-opening of the SVR. *(Author)*

**After a** major overhaul at Bridgnorth earlier in the year, former GWR 4-4-0 *City of Truro* runs into Highley Station on 28 September 1985. This was one of a number of visits this famous locomotive has made to the SVR. In complete contrast, on the adjacent road stands former LMS 'Jinty' 0-6-0 No. 47383, the SVR's fifth locomotive, which had arrived in the spring of 1968. *(Author)*

**The SVR** was one of the first preserved railways to run exclusive dining trains, *'The Severn Valley Limited'* evoking the GWR's *'Cornish Riviera Limited'*, the name officially bestowed in 1905 to the non-stop London, Paddington to Plymouth service. The style of cast headboard carried by *Erlestoke Manor* in this 2014 view of the SVR's *'Limited'*, entering Highley Station from the south, was styled on later BR, Western Region examples. *(Author)*

**Since the 1970s**, 'Santa Specials' have become an essential part of the SVR's calendar of special events. Five days before Christmas 2015, 4-6-0 No. 7802 *Bradley Manor* crosses Victoria Bridge, Arley, with one of those specials formed of seven restored LNER teak carriages, their occupants heading for an encounter with Father Christmas at Arley Station. *(Author)*

**The much-photographed** *Erlestoke Manor*, this time seen at the site of Kinlet Sidings hauling the 1.28pm from Kidderminster to Bridgnorth on 23 March 2014. Behind the engine are the SVR's rake of eight British Railways Mark I carriages, in the late-1950s livery of all-over maroon. *(Author)*

Light Railway Order (LRO) so that trains could be operated between Alveley and Foley Park, and in March the following year, this was transferred to the SVRC. A public service began to run between Bridgnorth and Highley in April, and then onwards to Bewdley in May. This extension immediately elevated the railway to the top of the railway preservation league table and when the loop was brought into use at Arley in May the following year it allowed the line to be used to its maximum capacity. The original McKenzie & Holland signalbox at Arley had been demolished in early preservation years, so it was the re-erected former London & North Western Railway (LNWR) signalbox from Yorton that was brought into use there in April 1976.

The next few years were ones of consolidation, during which time the Severn Valley Railway became a very popular and well-respected organisation. It is difficult in accounts such as this one to adequately acknowledge the amount of time and hard work put in by members of preserved railways. The public see the station staff, engine drivers and firemen, and perhaps the signalmen. But out of sight there are many more at work in offices, sheds and out on the track. Preservation cannot be sustained without continual maintenance. The headlines usually go to locomotive and then carriage restoration, but whole rakes of the latter have to be kept clean and tidy after each day's work as their condition leaves a lasting impression on the public, who probably spend most of their visit in these vehicles. Track has to be maintained and periodically renewed, trees and undergrowth kept under control, and the integrity of signalling guaranteed by regular inspection. And because the aim is to present the railway, visually and operationally, as it was in steam days at a time when labour was

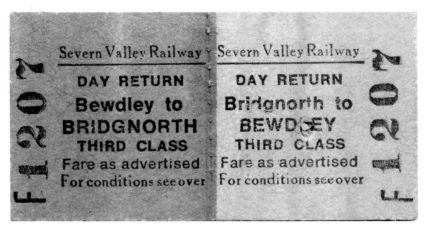

**Bridgnorth–Bewdley** day return ticket 1980. *(Author's collection)*

**When the SVR** took over at Bewdley, the signalling was intact and little modification was needed before steam trains could run once again in and out of the Station. In this photograph taken on 21 September 1986, 4-6-0 *Leander* pulls away from platform three with a train for Bridgnorth. *(Author)*

**All the signals** seen in the previous photograph are operated from Bewdley North signalbox, the interior of which appears in this 1984 photograph. The SVR inherited the lever frame, but fitted the electrical instruments and illuminated diagram with its own staff. The design of block instruments, repeaters and bells, dates back to the 1850s and 60s, all but the bells fitted with a single-needle movement patented in 1863 by E. Spagnoletti of the GWR. That movement became the standard in the majority of block instruments used throughout Britain. *(Author)*

**Bewdley North** signalbox can be seen in this view of the SVR's observation car leaving Bewdley at the rear of a train for Bridgnorth on 20 October 1985. Originally built in 1948 as an inspection carriage, it was privately purchased from British Rail and brought to the SVR in 1973, where it later became a popular vehicle, available to hire for special celebrations and occasions. *(Author)*

plentiful and cheap, the task is even more demanding.

In 1980, *'God's Wonderful Railway'*, filmed on the line, was broadcast on BBC TV, boosting passenger numbers to a record-breaking 180,000 by the end of the year at a time when the national economy was struggling. By then, the railway was undoubtedly one of the country's major tourist attractions and the old attitudes of the 'establishment' towards it had changed. In 1982, an agreement was signed with Shropshire County Council whereby the SVRHC would only have to find 30 per cent of the costs of building the new bypass bridge at Bridgnorth. The railway had become so important in the local economy that neither the county nor local authorities wanted to see it deprived of its northern terminus.

Having cast a shadow over the first fifteen years of the railway's life at Bridgnorth, the bridge was erected with

**A view** from Bewdley South signalbox in April 1983. The signalling here had not altered since British Rail ran the Station. The large, brick building on the left was the former goods shed in which many wagons have been restored for use on the SVR. *(Author)*

very little fuss during the winter of 1982/3, the SVRHC contributing £31,500 to a £105,000 contract. The bridge was ready for use when the new operating season began on 5 March 1983. At the end of the following month, however, part of the railway embankment immediately south of the bridge unexpectedly collapsed, halting services, but as if to underline the new rapprochement between the railway and the County Council, the latter immediately organised the necessary reinstatement, the railway being cleared of all responsibility for the slip. The line reopened on 18 May.

Only four days previously, British Rail had closed the goods yard at Kidderminster and this immediately triggered the SVRHC's next big project

**On 12 September 1982** a demonstration freight train crosses Victoria Bridge, Arley. Since the SVRHC took over responsibility for this structure in 1974, the deck has been completely replaced twice, first in 1979/80 and then again in 2004. In 1994 all layers of original and subsequent paint were grit blasted from all the metal parts and so that none of the mixture polluted the river below, the whole bridge was encased in plastic sheeting. Obviously, all this work has been costly, even with generous grants from English Heritage, and illustrates that there is much more to heritage railways than steam locomotives and special events. (Author)

– the extension of passenger services to Kidderminster. Negotiations with British Rail and outline planning had started in the late 1970s, but although it was a very ambitious scheme, it came at just the right time for the railway, when its reputation was high and the economy was beginning to boom. The aim was to purchase the line from the SVR's existing boundary at Foley Park, through to

Kidderminster Junction and to lease the redundant goods yard there on which a new terminus could be constructed. To raise the £300,000 required, a share issue was launched in November 1983 and such was the enthusiasm for the scheme amongst supporters of the railway, by the beginning of May the following year the whole amount had been secured with donations still being made.

Contractors had started work in the goods yard in March, and only four

The **SVRHC** is also responsible for a number of viaducts such as Oldbury Viaduct just south of Bridgnorth that was the focus of major repairs in 1975. In this photograph of that structure, ex-LMS 2-6-0 No 2968 makes an impressive sight with a southbound train on 26 December 2010. *(Adrian White)*

**The driver** of *Erlestoke Manor* looks down on the re-instated embankment immediately south of the new Bridgnorth Bypass Bridge, May 1983. *(Author)*

**For almost** exactly ten years between 1974 and 1984, Bewdley was the southern terminus for regular SVR passenger services to and from Bridgnorth. This meant that the locomotives of every train had to be detached and 'run round' ready for their return journeys. War Department 2-10-0 *Gordon* was undertaking that manoeuvre when photographed at Bewdley North in the summer of 1981. Twenty-seven years later, in July 2008, this engine was officially presented to the SVRHC from the National Army Museum. *(Author)*

months later, on 30 July 1984, the first passenger-carrying steam train pulled alongside a completely new island platform. Only four months later, the western section of a new brick terminal building was complete, followed by the opening on 28 September 1985 of the main entrance with booking hall, offices and the *'King & Castle'* pub. It had taken just 18 months from the first spade going in the ground to the opening of two-thirds of a replica of a late-nineteenth-century, brick-built, standard GWR station. It was a truly magnificent achievement, and unique in railway preservation at the time. The speed in which the site had been cleared and secured, track laid, buildings erected and a new timetable implemented, with all the attendant extra mileage, coal and water consumption of the locomotives, along with the additional staff required,

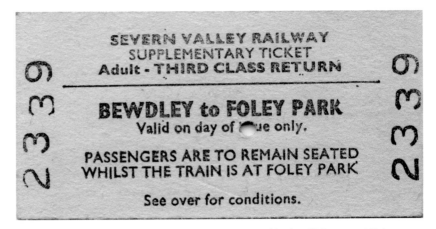

SEVERN VALLEY RAILWAY
SUPPLEMENTARY TICKET
Adult - THIRD CLASS RETURN

**BEWDLEY to FOLEY PARK**
Valid on day of issue only.

PASSENGERS ARE TO REMAIN SEATED
WHILST THE TRAIN IS AT FOLEY PARK

See over for conditions.

2339    2339

**In 1972** the SVRHC acquired the line between Alveley Sidings and Foley Park, and after a regular service had started running into Bewdley Station from May 1974, the SVR occasionally ran special shuttle trains between there and its boundary with British Rail at Foley Park. *(Author's collection)*

**A few weeks** before the SVRC extended its services beyond Bewdley to Kidderminster at the end of July 1984, the fireman of former GWR 0-6-0 No. 3205 hands over the Arley–Bewdley North single-line token to the signalman at the latter. Fourteen years earlier, on 23 May 1970, this locomotive had hauled the first SVRC-operated train out of Bridgnorth Station. *(Author)*

**The first amenities** at the new Kidderminster Terminus were very basic as this photograph, taken on 19 August 1984, shows. Such was the success of the fund raising, however, that new permanent buildings were quickly in place for the following season. *(Author)*

**Bridgnorth–Kidderminster** return ticket 1985. *(Author's collection)*

was not matched by any other equivalent organisation in the 1980s.

It was also fitting that the first full year of services to and from Kidderminster coincided with national celebrations to mark the 150th anniversary of the GWR. With money still being donated, the SVRHC was also able to purchase the former goods warehouse at Kidderminster (last used by Pickfords), and between March 1986 and December

1987 build, equip and commission a 62-lever signalbox close by. Once again, this was another first in railway preservation. On the other, western, side of the new station, the former GWR grain and wool warehouse of 1878 was taken over by a group of enthusiasts who formed a charitable trust to restore the building for use as a museum and archive, opening it as the Kidderminster Railway Museum in 1990.

As if to balance these successes, at the other end of the line, residents of a new housing estate recently constructed to the north-west of Bridgnorth Station, had obtained a court order in the spring of 1986 to prevent engine boilers being riveted in the open because of the noise nuisance this caused. The dispute rumbled on into the following year as the SVR drew up plans for a new building in which this work could be done. Another ban in November 1988 was imposed

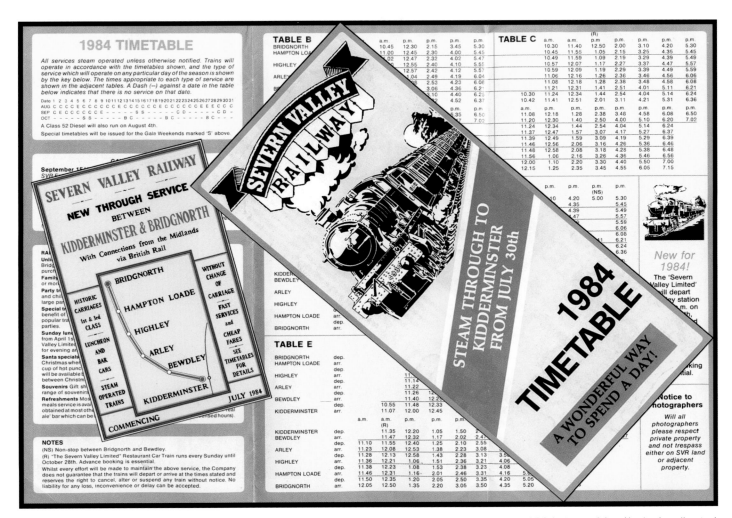

**1984 timetable.** *(Author's collection)*

**The main entrance** to Kidderminster Town Station, decorated for the 2013 season of Santa Specials. Great care was taken in 1984 to ensure this new Terminus was based on an authentic GWR structure. The station buildings at Ross-on-Wye were used as the template and replicated in almost every detail (except metric-sized bricks had to be used at Kidderminster!). Ross-on-Wye Station, opened in 1890, had been designed by J. E. Danks of the GWR's Civil Engineer's Department. *(Author)*

**After July 1984,** when trains began to run regularly through Bewdley Station, new locations were opened up for photographers, such as Bewdley South, seen here. The distant signals (those painted yellow) were added by the SVR's Signal & Telegraph (S&T) Department at the end of the 1989 season. *(Adrian White)*

before the new boiler shop was ready for use the following year.

In 1990 a record 213,029 visitors travelled on the railway, but despite this encouraging start and all the recent investment, the first few years of the new decade were a difficult time. In 1993, the SVRC had to dismiss its long-serving General Manager and within months was challenged by British Rail's announcement that it was to auction off the Kidderminster site on which the SVRHC had invested so much. Fortunately, the railway was

able to buy the leasehold and, in 1994, another successful share issue raised sufficient funds to cover the costs of this acquisition. In that same year there also occurred a Government initiative that was to have, arguably, the greatest impact for a generation on the development of museums, preserved railways and other 'heritage' attractions throughout the country. In 1994 the Heritage Lottery Fund (HLF) started to make grants available, and over the next two decades a huge mountain of applications were submitted for all manner of preservation, restoration and interpretation projects.

One of the first projects submitted to the HLF by the SVRHC was for the part-funding of a new building at Kidderminster capable of stabling fifty passenger carriages used regularly

As part of the celebrations for the 150th anniversary of the GWR in 1985, a replica of the first member of Daniel Gooch's famous class of 2-2-2-2 (usually designated 4-2-2) broad-gauge locomotives – *Iron Duke* built in 1847 – was created. The replica was steamed on a short section of track laid alongside The Albert Memorial in London, before visiting various heritage sites around the country. It is seen here at Bridgnorth in June 1985. *(Author)*

Just some of the thousands of items on display at the Kidderminster Railway Museum that won a Gulbenkian award in 1992 for 'outstanding improvements achieved with limited resources'. Since then, as well as objects, the museum has assembled a vast collection of photographic prints, negatives, glass plates and colour transparencies illustrating British railway history from the 1860s to the 1960s, copies of which are made available to enthusiasts and researchers. *(Author)*

**Two visiting** 'Deltic' diesel locomotives at Bridgnorth in October 1989 – no. D9016 'Gordon Highlander' on the right and no. D9000 'Royal Scots Grey' with the 'Flying Scotsman' (train) headboard, on the left. In the background to the left, is the SVRHC's newly completed brick and steel-clad boiler shop. *(Author)*

**Visiting locomotives** have always drawn enthusiasts to the SVR, and in March 2012, former LNER Class A4 4-6-2 No. 4464 *Bittern,* finished in its 1930s garter blue livery, was able to haul the SVR's rake of eight ex-LNER carriages, all in their 1930s varnished teak finish. The nostalgic, and at the time unique, combination is seen leaving Bridgnorth. That year, ownership of the carriages was transferred to the newly-created Severn Valley Railway Charitable Trust. *(Adrian White)*

**A view** from the guards van of a mixed -goods train consisting of restored wagons appropriately hauled by ex-GWR 2-8-0 No. 2857, every vehicle the result of hundreds of hours of hard work by volunteers over many years. (Adrian White)

**Ex-GWR 2-6-2T** No. 5164 enters Highley Station in August 2013 alongside the well-maintained, much-photographed and frequently-modelled McKenzie & Holland signalbox of 1883. (Author)

**Charging towards**
Arley on 23 March
2014 with the
11.45am from
Bridgnorth, 1929-built
GWR 4-6-0 No. 4936
*Kinlet Hall* was within
a few miles of the
location from which
it took its name.
Compared to other
steam locomotives,
*Kinlet Hall* was a late
restoration project,
being rescued from
Barry Scrapyard
in 1981 and only
returning to steam in
2000. *(Author)*

**Former LNER Class K4** 2-6-0 No. 3442 *The Great Marquess* became a familiar sight on the SVR, working intermittently on the line between 1972 and 2005. After a major overhaul it is seen here emerging from Bewdley Tunnel in 1989 with a northbound train. *(Author's collection)*

**Visiting steam locomotive** 4-6-2 No. 71000 *Duke of Gloucester* making its presence smelt north of Arley in May 2009. It was rescued from Barry Scrapyard by a group of enthusiasts in 1974 minus its three cylinders, valve gear and connecting rods. At the time the accepted wisdom was that it would be impossible to cast new cylinders and fabricate new parts for the running gear. But that was achieved, and in 1986 'The Duke' was steamed again at the Great Central Railway's Loughborough site. *(Author)*

**The DMU Group** (West Midlands) was formed in 1989 to preserve an example of one of the last British Railways DMUs that were being taken out of service at the time. Leading this formation, photographed just north of Arley in February 2016, is Driving Motor Composite No. 52064, built in 1958 and brought to the SVR in working order in 1990. The use of DMUs evokes the final years of British Railways' operation of the line. *(Author)*

throughout the season. The initial submission made in 1996 was for a traditional GWR-style brick building to match those at the station, but before the project could proceed, these ambitious plans had to be modified so that what the HLF finally provided £1.75m towards was a steel-framed and sheet-clad structure. The ceremonial first sod was cut on 28 July 1999 and the contractors handed over the completed building on 20 April 2000.

The following month the SVRC could boast that it had been running steam trains along the Severn Valley for thirty years, twice as long as British Railways. It had not been an inevitable progression to fame and certainly not to fortune, but the railway was at the very least still operational, and passenger numbers were beginning to recover to over 200,000 per annum. In those thirty years, inevitably, the emphasis on various aspects of the railway's operations had changed, as had the expectations of those visiting the line and making use of its facilities. The running of large, ex-main line locomotives – both steam and diesel – attracted the visitors, but was considered by some purists as out of keeping with a rural branch

line. Special events, the hiring out of trains and stations for corporate events and weddings, helped the coffers, but would have been unthinkable to the SVR management in its Edwardian heyday. Gradually, inevitably in purely financial terms, the SVR had progressed from a nineteenth-century speculative venture, through a late-twentieth-century 'preserved' railway to a twenty-first-century 'heritage' attraction with all the compromises that entailed.

Completed within a couple of years of each other in the first decade of the twenty-first century, there were two projects that illustrated very clearly

**The impressive** 1999/2000 carriage shed on the southern approaches to Kidderminster Town Station. In this photograph taken in September 2013, former GWR 2-6-2T No. 5164 passes with a short, local train from Bewdley. This locomotive was another 1970s escapee from Barry Scrapyard, re-entering traffic on the SVR in 1979. *(Author)*

the changes of approach to presenting the railway to the public. The first represented the traditional face of preservation, a desire to turn the clock back and immerse the visitor in an environment from the past, whilst the second represented a new desire to offer a visitor attraction to compete with places such as the Ironbridge Gorge Museum.

After the impressively rapid erection

**The lovingly-restored** GWR 'Pul-syn-etic' station clock originally located at Wolverhampton and currently hanging from the 2006 overall roof at Kidderminster Town station. *(Author)*

cast-iron and steel skeleton of the overall roof was erected. By April almost all the glazing had been installed and this was quickly followed by construction of the new eastern wing in brickwork that matched the 1985 buildings. By September, all was complete, with the restaurant open to the public.

In complete contrast, and under development at the same time, was 'The Engine House' just to the south of Highley Station. This represented the 'alternative' approach to heritage interpretation. The idea of having a building where engines waiting their turn to be repaired or overhauled could be displayed for the public went back to the earliest days of the SVRC. In 1973 there had been plans for 'Heavy Maintenance Storage' covered accommodation and a turntable on the site of the National Coal Board's (NCB) land sale yard at Highley. Nothing came of this scheme, but when the opportunity arose to match HLF money with funds available from the European Regional Development Fund and Advantage West Midlands, it was decided this was to be the location for an uncompromisingly modern building, not just for the display of static engines, but to include a museum exhibition and facilities for educational groups and meetings, as well as a café and shop. The project had much in common with many of the recent huge, multi-million-pound schemes being undertaken by the nearby Ironbridge Gorge Museum Trust and which were funded in the same way. The Highley site was purchased in August 2001; three years later planning permission was granted for a £4.5m scheme and as the structure began to take shape, the SVRHC launched its own appeal and share issue for additional money.

The Engine House was not only a controversial addition to the landscape; its fitting out and public opening were

of two-thirds of the new replica station at Kidderminster in 1985, the final one-third of the Terminus to house the catering facility had remained only an aspiration for the next twenty years. Also in abeyance was the plan to cover with a glazed canopy the circulating area created between these buildings and the island platform. In the end, the canopy was erected first, a little ahead of the eastern range of brick buildings. In January 2006, the temporary 1985 buffet was demolished and in February the

**The uncompromisingly** twenty-first-century building that is 'The Engine House' at Highley. Its design, and the way the contents were displayed, resulted from the deliberate intention of SVRHC management to widen the appeal of the railway so that it could compete with other family-oriented visitor attractions. *(Author)*

**One of** the displays within 'The Engine House' at Highley. This style of exhibition had evolved with the 'new museum movement' of the 1970s, and had become familiar to visitors to places such as 'ThinkTank' at Birmingham and in some of the Ironbridge Gorge Museum Trust's sites in Coalbrookdale. It is probably fair to say it was not liked by those who mourned the closure of the old Birmingham Science Museum in 1997, but was celebrated by those who supported 'ThinkTank' as its 2001 replacement. *(Author)*

**The aftermath** of the torrential rains of 19 June 2007 at the south end of Highley Station. *(SVRHC)*

**The result** of just one culvert close to Borle Brook Viaduct that was unable to cope with the 19 June 2007 downpours. The stretch of water at the top of the picture is not the River Severn, but the lake formed by the flood water. The river is out of view, top left. *(SVRHC)*

delayed by the biggest disaster to befall the railway. During the night of 19 June 2007, when the equivalent of two weeks' worth of rain fell in just half an hour, embankments were washed out at numerous locations along the railway, creating serious breaches in the line. The result was a nine-month closure whilst extensive repairs had to be carried out that eventually cost over £3.5m. Tremendous support was forthcoming from the three funders of the 'Engine House' project, as well as from Bridgnorth District Council, the Wyre Forest District Council, other heritage railways and preservation groups, contractors and the general public. The first train to traverse the reinstated line between Kidderminster and Bridgnorth ran on 20 March 2008, the same day 'The Engine House' was officially opened. The following day, Good Friday, the familiar, annual intensive Bank Holiday public timetable was back in action.

The hard work and determination of everyone involved in reinstating earthworks, track and signalling was fittingly acknowledged with three awards and a Royal visit. The visit of HRH The Prince of Wales and HRH The Duchess of Cornwall took place on 10 June 2008. It had, of course, been arranged long before the disaster, but nevertheless it became a celebration of the line's reopening. A few days later, on 25 June, the SVRHC Chairman was presented with the Transport Trust's 'Preservationist of the Year' award, immediately accepting it on behalf of all shareholders, members, staff and volunteers of the railway. On 11 November the railway was awarded 'Best Tourism Experience of the Year' by the Heart of England Tourist Board, and finally on 3 December 2008, it received

**Highley's 2009 footbridge** framing rebuilt Bullied 4-6-2 No. 34053 *Sir Keith Park* entering Highley Station on 2 November 2014. Named after the Air Chief Marshal who played such a significant role in Fighter Command and then the defence of Malta during the Second World War, the engine had been working on the SVR for two and a half years. *(Author)*

Ian Allan Publishing's 'Independent Railway of the Year' award.

The final element of the Engine House project was the erection of a footbridge at Highley Station so that passengers visiting the new attraction did not have to use the barrow crossing at the south end of the platform. The new bridge was fabricated with a welded-steel lattice so that it closely resembled the structure erected by the GWR immediately before the First World War that had been dismantled for scrap in 1974. The Duke of Gloucester officially opened the new bridge on 21 October 2009.

Buoyed by the success of all this new work at Highley and Kidderminster, and

particularly by the goodwill displayed by all parts of the heritage and local communities during the disaster of 2007, the SVRHC decided to celebrate the 150th anniversary of the opening of the line in 1862 by another major share issue. Launched on 1 October 2012, the aim was to raise £3m towards a portfolio of projects, ranging from the restoration of GWR 4-6-0 No. 4930 *Hagley Hall*, through essential infrastructure maintenance to a complete redevelopment of Bridgnorth Station. This latter project was christened 'SteamWorks' and was to involve the erection of a number of steel, glass and timber-clad buildings in the same twenty-first-century style as those forming 'The Engine House' at Highley. There was also to be an additional footbridge next to the signalbox that would lead straight into a new high-level viewing gallery in the locomotive shed. Money immediately began to roll in for this bold revamp, but so too did considerable opposition to

**The view** from the footbridge at Highley on 23 March 2014 looking southwards as ex-GWR 0-6-0T No. 6435, visiting from the Bodmin & Wenford Railway, enters the loop with its autocoach (or autotrailer), passing ex-GWR 2-8-0 No. 2857 waiting to leave with an early afternoon train for Kidderminster. Restoration of the autocoach was completed at Bewdley in 2011, and during the final painting, it was named *Chaffinch* as intended when the coach was turned out new from Swindon Works in 1954. *(Author)*

**Visiting locomotive,** ex-Southern Railway 4-4-0 No. 925 *Cheltenham*, passing Kidderminster Town signalbox in September 2013. The signalbox was erected in 1986 and commissioned in December the following year with a 62-lever frame recovered from Acton Yard signalbox. In the background is the former GWR goods warehouse, acquired by the SVRHC for the restoration of carriages. *(Author)*

the plans expressed on web-based social media sites.

Over the next few weeks, critics gained widespread support for their view that the new development would completely compromise the site at Bridgnorth with its Listed Grade II station building and was far removed from the spirit of heritage preservation for which they believed the SVR had always stood. Before long, opponents were rallying around a Bridgnorth 'Plan B' that put SVRHC management in a

very embarrassing position. Fortunately, sensible counsel within the railway was able to suggest a strategy that would both address the critics' concerns and allow the formulation of new plans that all parties could rally around. To this end, a Conservation & Heritage

Committee was set up with a remit to review this and future developments, as well as award small grants to ensure heritage throughout the railway was not compromised on the grounds of cost, for example, when it was cheaper, but not appropriate, to replace cast-iron guttering with PVC.

The new committee was quick to issue a press release announcing its new role within the SVR and its intention to revisit Bridgnorth's SteamWorks project. Social media criticism subsided.

In the following months, meetings were held, interested parties consulted, and gradually the operational requirements at Bridgnorth to meet the needs of passengers and staff, combined with the aim of preserving and enhancing the existing heritage, led to new plans. Original drawings and photographs of numerous authentic GWR buildings were used to create the designs of the new structures (as had been the case with the Kidderminster Station project in 1984); all this work progressed in

**Suitably finished** in its original 1936 livery of apple green when it visited in 2007, LNER Class V2 No. 4771 *Green Arrow* was another authentic match for the SVR's rake of LNER teak carriages. It was photographed making an effortless exit from Bewdley Tunnel during its stay. Retired the following year, its owners, the NRM, whilst spending millions of pounds returning *Flying Scotsman* to steam, seem unwilling to consider anything other than cosmetic restoration for *Green Arrow*. (Adrian White)

close consultation with English Heritage and the local authorities. By the end of 2015, all was in place for a phased project starting with the erection of new refreshment and toilet facilities where the shed for the Wolverhampton–Bridgnorth bus had once stood, and then the restoration of the original station building. With the money that had been raised in 2012 having already been partially spent on *Hagley Hall* and infrastructure projects, another share issue was launched in November 2016 to finance completion of the work at Bridgnorth. At the time of writing, all the phases there are yet to be completed, but by the time this book appears in print, a start will have been made and the SVR should be looking forward to continuing its challenging mission to preserve the past and present it in an authentic, but engaging way for future generations.

**Part of** the interior of the impressive Kidderminster Carriage Works. Since it was acquired by the SVRHC in 1985, equipment has been brought in to enable passenger coaches to be completely refurbished, from underframes, body work and upholstery to final painting. *(Author)*

**A view** looking south from Kidderminster Town Station with the ex-OW&WR main line in the background on the left and the unforgiving bulk of the Kidderminster Diesel Depot on the right. Undercover accommodation for the fleet of diesels used on the SVR had long been an aspiration for the groups owning the locomotives. Fund raising began in earnest in 1996, but it was not until the start of 2015 that sufficient finance was available for construction to start. Erection and fitting out with an overhead travelling crane was rapid and a formal opening took place on 20 May 2016 during a Diesel Gala weekend. *(Author)*

**Between 1994 and 2008,** a significant piece of railway history was made when an LNER Class A1 4-6-2 locomotive was constructed from scratch. Christened *Tornado* and numbered 60163 as though it was simply the next in the original class of 49 engines that had appeared between 1948 and 1949, it immediately captured the attention of media and general public alike. It has visited the SVR on a number of occasions, this photograph taken on 11 October 2015 at Northwood on the approach to Bewdley. *(Author)*

**Since the 1980s,** special events have become vital for all heritage railways in order to attract new visitors and encourage existing enthusiasts to return. During the SVR's Spring Gala of 20 and 21 March 2015, former GWR 2-6-2 No. 4566 was in action, and, at the end of the last busy day, was photographed hurrying out of Bewdley towards Kidderminster. *(Andy Lock)*

# Bibliography

The following is not a definitive list of all the books that have been written about the Severn Valley Railway, but a list of those used as references in the compilation of this book:

'Great Western Locomotives on the Severn Valley', Tony Barfield, Severn
    Valley Railway News, No. 25, Autumn 1972, pp12–15

'The West Midlands Lines of the Great Western Railway',
    K. M. Beck, Ian Allan Publishing, 1983

'The Tenbury & Bewdley Railway', Keith Beddoes & William H. Smith, Wild Swan, 1995

'Rail Centres: Wolverhampton', Paul Collins, Ian Allan Publishing, 1990

'Track Layout Diagrams of the Great Western Railway, Section 32,
    East Shropshire', 2nd edition. R. A. Cooke, 1994

'The Severn Valley Railway at Arley', Wild Swan, Barrie Geens, revised edition, 1995

'The Severn Valley, Handy Aids No. 7', Great Western
    Railway, 1st edition, 1913, (2nd edition 1923)

'Register of Closed Railways 1948–1991', G. Hurst, Milepost, 1992

'The Severn Valley Railway', John Marshall, David St John Thomas, 1989

'Rail Centres: Shrewsbury', Richard K. Morriss, Ian Allan Publishing, 1986

'A Short History of William Exley & Sons', A. J. Mugridge, published by the author, 1997

'Severn Valley Steam', Sir Gerald Nabarro MP, Routledge & Kegan Paul, 1971

*'The Severn Valley Railway'*, D. J. Smith, Town & Country Press, 1968

*'Ironbridge and The Electric Revolution'*, Michael Stratton, John Murray in association with National Power, 1994

*'The Billingsley and Kinlet Railways'*, John Tennant, *Severn Valley Railway News*, No. 24, Summer 1972, pp23–27

*'Barges & Bargemen: a Social History of the Upper Severn Navigation 1660–1900'*, Barrie Trinder, Phillimore, 2005

*'The Industrial Revolution in Shropshire'*, Barrie Trinder, Phillimore, 1973

*'Severn Valley Railway: A View from the Past'*, M. A. Vanns, Shrewdale Publishing, 2013

# Index